Marian Cox

Hamlet

William Shakespeare

Philip Allan Updates, an imprint of Hodder Education, part of Hachette Livre UK, Market Place, Deddington, Oxfordshire OX15 0SE

Orders

Bookpoint Ltd, 130 Milton Park, Abingdon, Oxfordshire, OX14 4SB
tel: 01235 827720
fax: 01235 400454
e-mail: uk.orders@bookpoint.co.uk
Lines are open 9.00 a.m.–5.00 p.m., Monday to Saturday, with a 24-hour message answering service. You can also order through the Philip Allan Updates website: www.philipallan.co.uk

ISBN 978-1-84489-604-2

Printed in Malta

Hachette Livre UK's policy is to use papers that are natural, renewable and recyclable products and made from wood grown in sustainable forests. The logging and manufacturing processes are expected to conform to the environmental regulations of the country of origin.

P01321

Contents

Introduction

Aims of the guide

The purpose of this Student Text Guide to *Hamlet* is to enable you to organise your thoughts and responses to the play, to deepen your understanding of key features and aspects, and finally to help you to address the particular requirements of examination questions in order to obtain the best possible grade. It will also prove useful to those writing a coursework piece on the play by providing a number of summaries, lists, analyses and references to help with the content and construction of the assignment.

It is assumed that you have read and studied the play already under the guidance of a teacher or lecturer. This is a revision guide, not an introduction, although some of its content serves the purpose of providing initial background. It can be read in its entirety in one sitting, or it can be dipped into and used as a reference guide to specific and separate aspects of the play.

The *Text Guidance* section consists of a series of subsections which examine key aspects of the play including contexts, scene summaries, themes and imagery; they also discuss interpretations and controversies. Emboldened terms within the Text Guidance section are glossed in 'Literary terms and concepts' on pp. 103–08.

The final section, *Questions and Answers*, gives examples of essay questions of different types, and includes mark schemes, exemplar essay plans and samples of marked work.

Line references in this guide refer to the *Penguin Shakespeare* edition of the play.

Assessment Objectives

The Assessment Objectives for A-level English Literature are common to all boards:

AO1	communicate clearly the knowledge, understanding and insight appropriate to literary study, using appropriate terminology and accurate and coherent written expression
AO2i	respond with knowledge and understanding to literary texts of different types and periods
AO2ii	respond with knowledge and understanding to literary texts of different types and periods, exploring and commenting on relationships and comparisons between literary texts
AO3	show detailed understanding of the ways in which writers' choices of form, structure and language shape meanings

AO4	articulate independent opinions and judgements, informed by different interpretations of literary texts by other readers
AO5i	show understanding of the contexts in which literary texts are written and understood
AO5ii	evaluate the significance of cultural, historical and other contextual influences on literary texts and study

A summary of each Assessment Objective is given below and would be worth memorising:

AO1	clarity of written communication (accuracy and expression)
AO2	informed personal response in relation to time and genre (literary context)
AO3	the creative literary process (context of writing)
AO4	critical and interpretative response (context of reading)
AO5	evaluation of influences (cultural context)

It is essential that you pay close attention to the Assessment Objectives, and their weighting, for the board for which you are entered. These are what the examiner will be looking for, and you must address them *directly* and *specifically*, in addition to proving general familiarity with and understanding of the text, and being able to present an argument clearly, relevantly and convincingly.

Remember that the examiners are seeking above all else evidence of an informed personal response to the text. A revision guide such as this can help you to understand the text and to form your own opinions, and can suggest areas to think about, but it cannot replace your own ideas and responses as an individual reader.

Text Guidance

LITERATURE

Hamlet

Contexts

The England of 1600 was about to undergo a radical change of monarch and was involved in ambitious ventures of discovery and colonial expansion. The new century brought challenges to the Elizabethan world view, which had been inherited from the Middle Ages; and this conflict is represented in the drama of the period. Below are some of the contemporary religious beliefs and social attitudes which throw light on the hopes, fears, thoughts and actions of the characters in *Hamlet*. Shakespeare exploits them while simultaneously calling them into question.

Cultural context

Chain of being

The Elizabethans inherited from medieval theology the concept of a hierarchical chain of being. Every creature appeared on this in its ordained position on a ladder descending from God through angel, king, man and woman (in that order) to animal, vegetable and finally mineral. It is necessary to know about this belief in a divine order to appreciate the objection to women ruling men. It also explains why it was believed that failure to apply reason reduced humans to the animal state of being governed by appetite and instinct. In Shakespeare a human who falls below the level of man into the realm of bestiality is labelled a monster. Hamlet finds it difficult to reconcile himself to man's place on the chain: although in the likeness of an angel, man is really a lowly and mortal sinner with all the ills that flesh is heir to.

Microcosm and macrocosm

The **microcosm/macrocosm** medieval theory still influential in Shakespeare's time was that the king, ruled by reason, was the head and centre of the body politic (i.e. the state). If he gave way to passion or misjudgement the consequences would ripple outwards like a stone thrown into a pond, causing a breakdown of normal relations at every level: family, court, state. 'Something is rotten in the state of Denmark' because there is a 'dram of evil', a licentiousness unable to resist temptation, in the soul of Claudius, who is called, as all kings were, by the name of the country he represented. At the time a king was believed to have a 'divine right' to rule, that is, to have been appointed by God and to be superior to normal mortals. Therefore, the killing or usurping of a king was considered a grave offence which attracted devastating consequences for the whole country.

Nature

The ubiquitous presence of the word 'nature' in Elizabethan literature, in addition to **imagery** deriving from it and arguments about it, stems from the contemporary debate about the definition of nature, which has two contradictory aspects: the benevolent and harmonious, and the chaotic and destructive. Shakespeare's characters examine the **paradox** of God's creation containing poison and 'cankers', and the existence of unnatural monsters, which could only have been bred by nature and must, therefore, be natural in some sense. His plays also examine closely the concept of human nature and its relationship to nature as a whole; in both there is evil and disease.

Appearance

External appearance was believed in the medieval period to be an indicator of what lay within (i.e. goodness or evil). A physical deformity was thought to be the devil's mark and took many women to the stake. This was being questioned by Shakespeare's time, and appearance versus reality is a central issue in *Hamlet*, where the imagery of 'seeming' permeates the language of the play. If appearances, which are all we have to go on, are deceptive, and therefore character judgement is false, knowledge erroneous and truth elusive, then one cannot be sure of anything. This is the conundrum that torments many of Shakespeare's tragic heroes. The ghost would look like his father whether he really were his ghost or whether he were an evil spirit luring Hamlet to his damnation, for 'one may smile, and smile, and be a villain'. Women were commonly satirised for their vanity at this time, and their practice of face-painting was condemned as a disguise to deceive men.

Reason

The failure of reason was considered to be the cause of the Fall of Man (Adam allowed his love for Eve to overrule his better judgement and obedience to God). Elizabethans therefore believed it was dangerous to let reason be dominated by passion. Characters in Shakespeare who become uncontrollably emotional are heading for a fall, as their intellect is what makes them human (superior to beasts) and keeps them sane. In a state of heightened passion, such as anger or jealousy, mistakes are made, impulses are activated without sufficient reflection to moderate them, and one is no longer in control of oneself or of the situation. Hamlet admires Horatio for not being 'passion's slave' and he himself vacillates between 'blood and judgement'.

The seven deadly sins

The **seven deadly sins** of the medieval church were pride, envy, gluttony (greed for food), lechery (lust), avarice (greed for money), wrath (anger), sloth (laziness). These vices (which can be identified in literary works until the nineteenth century) were the foundation of morality in the medieval and Elizabethan/Jacobean periods. They feature as a masque in Marlowe's *Doctor Faustus*, for instance. Shakespeare employs them to suggest the faults of his villains; Claudius is guilty of envy, gluttony, and lechery. These mortal sins, most of which were thought to lead on to murder, were believed to consign one's soul to hell without further ado.

Spirits

Evil spirits were believed by Protestants (including James I, author of *Demonologie*) to be ever within earshot, and on the watch for an opportunity to corrupt and snatch a human soul from the pathway of righteousness. Ghosts were believed to be a deception of the devil. Characters in Shakespeare who are foolish, **hubristic** or tempted enough to invoke or give credence to spirit devils from murky depths are sealing their own damnation. Hamlet fears that this will be the outcome of heeding the ghost's admonitions. Catholics, however, believed that ghosts were the spirits of the departed, who returned in order to disclose a crime, and that it was a religious duty to help them find rest.

Suicide

The church did not distinguish between deliberate suicide and accidental self-slaughter. It believed that by definition the act denoted a state of being 'of unsound mind' and proved that the victim had fallen into the sin of despair (lack of hope, and therefore lack of belief in Christ's mercy) as a consequence of listening to evil spirits. Suicide was self-murder and therefore counter to God's will and human prerogative. (Until 1961 it was a criminal offence in the UK and an unsuccessful attempt could result in arrest.) Suicides were therefore not permitted to be buried in the hallowed ground of churchyards, as their souls had gone to hell.

Heaven, hell and purgatory

Hell was typically portrayed in plays and paintings as a region below the earth inhabited by tormented souls, some of whom were allowed to walk the earth between midnight and dawn if they had a message to communicate to the living. The medieval Catholic church taught (and still teaches) about the afterlife that those who had committed mortal (damnable) sins went straight to hell if they had not repented before death. Although there is no biblical basis for purgatory, it also taught that the souls of the departed who had committed venial (pardonable) sins for which they had not shown repentance or received absolution had to suffer for a time until purged (cleansed), before then being received into heaven when lightened of their burden of unabsolved sins. Protestants did not believe in the existence of purgatory. Sudden death was feared at the time *Hamlet* was set because if there was 'no shriving time allowed' then the soul would not be in a state of grace and fit for passage to heaven, since the last rites of confession, absolution, communion and anointing could not be administered.

Another relevant aspect of preparation for death was to beg forgiveness of anyone who might have a grudge against you (especially if you were an executioner), and it is therefore important that Laertes and Hamlet should swap forgiveness for each other's deaths before they expire in the final scene of the play.

Black and white

Black was traditionally the colour of death and of the devil, according to both biblical and mythological **sources**, and white was synonymous with the pure and good. For Elizabethans the word 'fair' meant both light-coloured and honest, and 'foul' was associated with darkness and evil. In the book of Genesis God declared 'Let there be Light' to bring truth and beauty into the world. An absence or putting out of light meant a **symbolic** return to chaos and descent into hell or the grave. Black is also associated with melancholy and grief, as well as revenge, and therefore this 'nighted colour' is Hamlet's adopted hue. There are several references in *Hamlet* to the colour 'sable', the heraldic word for black.

Melancholy

Shakespeare was familiar with at least one treatise on melancholia, a disease which was believed to be caused by an excess of black bile (which is the meaning of the word), and which was known as the Elizabethan malady. Timothy Bright's *Treatise of Melancholy* (1586) is echoed a number of times in the play. Melancholy was thought to lead to madness or to present it as a symptom. Hamlet's fondness for black clothing, looking downwards and feeling dull, heavy and earthbound are all indicators of his being afflicted with melancholy, which Claudius and Gertrude urge him to cast off.

Chastity

The security of society and peace of mind of men was dependent upon women's virginity before marriage — making them a bargaining tool for advantageous marriages to benefit the father's social status — and chastity after it, meaning faithfulness to their husbands. In a society which passes inheritance down the male line men needed to be sure that their son was really their own and not someone else's bastard, and a man's reputation would be destroyed by an unfaithful wife. Virginity and chastity were linked to religion via the Virgin Mary and regarded not only as an ideal state for women but as a test of the nobility of males, since only the higher orders were thought to be able to resist the temptations of the flesh; hence Hamlet's disgust at the sexual antics of his mother and his uncle in 'the rank sweat of an enseamèd bed'.

Incest

Marriage to one's brother's wife became a prohibited degree of closeness — and therefore counted as incest — according to a law of 1563, which followed the *Book of Common Prayer*'s 'Table of Kindred and Affinity' (1549) in saying that 'A woman may not marry with her...husband's brother'. This prohibition was based on the book of Leviticus, chapter 18, verse 16, and chapter 20, verse 21, but caused division in the church because of a contradiction in Deuteronomy. This was exploited by Henry VIII when he gained papal permission to marry Katherine of Aragon, widow of his brother Arthur, which the audience of *Hamlet* would have been aware of (and of the failure of the marriage to produce children). However, only the Ghost and Hamlet seem concerned about the charge of incest in the play, although for the rest of the characters it would have been expedient or diplomatic to ignore it.

Fickleness

The idea of the faithless female was a classical literary stereotype fostered by the medieval church, whose own misogyny was founded on the premise that Eve betrayed her husband and all mankind when she allowed herself to be seduced by a smooth-talking serpent — with which Claudius can be compared. Fickle fortune was iconographically represented as a blindfolded woman with a wheel which she turned at random, sending those in high positions plunging down. Hamlet draws upon this stereotype of inconstancy when he declares that 'Frailty, thy name is woman', in denouncing his mother for not remembering or mourning his father for long enough, and when he refers to the brevity of 'woman's love'.

Role of women

Women were possessions financially dependent on their fathers, to whom they owed obedience and domestic labour until they were handed over to the rule of their husbands, whom they had to love, honour and obey as well as giving them conjugal rights. The consequences of not performing these daughterly and wifely duties were serious: being disowned and deprived of a home, financial support and a place in society. Ophelia has no option but to obey her father's (and brother's) commands. According to the medieval chain of being still given credence at this time, women came below men on the hierarchy of creation, since it was believed that they were of inferior intellect and moral understanding to men. They could not bear arms or hold military rank or public office, and it was therefore unacceptable for them to attempt to dominate or overrule their husbands (a crime punishable by the ducking-stool at best and a witch trial at worst). Women could rise only through their association with men and their rank, hence Gertrude's need to secure her status as queen by marrying the next king.

The words used to define women, then and now, all relate to their sexual, and therefore financial, relationship with men: virgin, wife, widow, whore. Women rarely remarried at the time — and then only for political reasons — and certainly not until after a decent and fixed period of mourning of at least a year had elapsed. The church did not consider it desirable for women to remarry, at whatever age, and it was generally considered unnecessary and inappropriate for women beyond child-bearing age to do so.

The succession

The succession to the throne in medieval and **Renaissance** Europe was by elective, not hereditary, monarchy. Primogeniture (accession to the throne of the eldest son) was sometimes the determining factor, but this was not automatic (hence Macbeth's hopes) and the strongest male, the one best able to protect the kingdom, was the natural choice. Nomination came through the voice of the present (often dying) king in public (which is how Fortinbras becomes King of Denmark, since Hamlet is King at that moment of acclamation). Old Hamlet died suddenly, presumably before nominating a successor, leaving the field free for Claudius to claim the throne before anyone else (as Macbeth does after Duncan's death and the defection of Malcolm) with the support of the widow. As a younger son, Claudius has the common grievance of biblical, historical and fictional characters over the centuries (e.g. Edmund in *King Lear*) who have less power and status than their elder brothers and no prospects of inheritance, discriminated against purely because they are not the first-born.

Renaissance man

Hamlet is arguably the type of the perfect Renaissance man, the ideal to which young noblemen of the period aspired (personified by Sir Walter Raleigh among others), who had to be a poet, courtier, scholar, soldier, philosopher and lover. These attributes were believed to raise man to his highest level physically, intellectually and spiritually, to make him a paragon of all the manly virtues and a 'rose of the fair state'. Hamlet is deeply disappointed and cast down by the failure of others to live up to this ideal because of their limitations caused by foolishness, ignorance or corruption.

University of Wittenberg

The University of Wittenberg in Germany was not founded until 1502, 500 years after the period in which *Hamlet* is actually set. The sons of European nobility studied there, until an advanced age in some cases, to prepare for public office while waiting to inherit positions on the death of their fathers. It was the favourite university of Danes studying abroad. The curriculum took at least six years to cover and consisted of the trivium and the quadrivium, which were grammar, **rhetoric**, and logic, followed by arithmetic, geometry, music and astronomy. All of these were preparation for the study of philosophy and theology. Students typically entered at the age of 14, and if they wished to complete a doctorate had to stay for 18 years. Wittenberg was a famously Protestant university in Shakespeare's time, associated with Martin Luther, and had already been used as the setting for Marlowe's *Doctor Faustus* (1592). Paris was another university town, though it is not suggested that Laertes is pursuing specifically academic studies there. It does not help the problem of determining Hamlet's age that he wishes to return to study at Wittenberg (see note in the Arden Shakespeare edition of the play, p. 174).

Danegeld

Danegeld (literally 'Danish money') was a substantial annual tax in silver coins exacted by the King of Denmark from England in return for not attacking the country, as the Vikings had done sporadically throughout the tenth and eleventh centuries. Danegeld and hostilities between Denmark and England came to an end after the Norman invasion in 1066, therefore *Hamlet* must be set before this date. Claudius refers to recent attacks on England by 'the Danish sword' in Act IV scene 3 when he gives his reason for believing that the King of England will obey his command for the 'present death of Hamlet' in the letter he is sending with Rosencrantz and Guildenstern.

Elements and humours

The medieval world view still being given some credence in the late sixteenth and early seventeenth centuries was that just as the universe was composed of the four elements, humans, as representing the world in miniature, were composed of four humours relating to them, and the imbalance of the mixture created temperament and explained the differences in human personality. Astrologists attempted to explain the connection between the movements of the stars and events on earth by linking planets with their influences.

Fire	Mars	Summer	Hot & dry	Yellow bile (spleen)	Choleric (angry)
Air	Jupiter	Spring	Hot & wet	Blood (heart)	Sanguine (happy)
Water	Moon	Winter	Cold & wet	Phlegm (brain)	Phlegmatic (calm)
Earth	Saturn	Autumn	Cold & dry	Black bile (liver)	Melancholy (sad)

Theatrical context

Shakespeare's London

Shakespeare's company was feeling the competition of child actors at the rival Blackfriars theatre at this time, hence Hamlet's satire of them in Act II scene 2. He also refers to a 'late innovation' (perhaps a reference to the Essex rebellion of February 1601) which had caused the closure of the theatres and forced the players to become peripatetic. London was on edge at the turn of the century, because of the decline of the monarch who had reigned for over 40 years (from 1558) and the uncertainty about the future because of the problematic succession, threat of Spanish invasion and danger of a coup.

In the sixteenth and seventeenth centuries the theatre reflected the brutality, violence and disease of the London streets and emphasised the 'gross' and the 'rank'; the horror, death and pain contained in the action of plays was strongly contrasted with the gilded finery of the costumes, just as in the city the majestic and spectacular were juxtaposed with the garbage and stink of the streets and their sewers, the grand public arenas with the furtive alleys. One must remember that sudden and violent death from crime or disease was commonplace and people rarely lived to be 40. They lived in close contact with the death of relatives and the consciousness of their own mortality, and were well aware of the negative aspects of female sexuality — the opposite of the production of noble heirs to the kingdom and estates — in the whores and brothels which were part of everyday scenery and could not be ignored. Furthermore, spies were everywhere, and unorthodoxy of religion or sexuality was dangerous and often fatal, as one of Shakespeare's fellow playwrights, Christopher Marlowe, discovered. These social realities of contemporary life in the capital are all evident in *Hamlet*, despite its setting in a remote palace on the northern coast of Denmark many centuries before.

In the early seventeenth century, when Shakespeare wrote his major tragedies, drama had generally become more political, satirical, violent and tragic compared to the more lyrical tastes and pastoral works of the Elizabethans. There was a growing fashion for the use of masque and spectacle in plays and poetry, and a tendency among fellow playwrights such as Ben Jonson and John Webster to write bloodthirsty revenge tragedies in urban settings. However, wit, **irony** and sophistication of ideas were still paramount in the plots, characterisation and language of the theatre.

Play-going appealed to all sections of the population; the poor stood as 'groundlings' in the 'pit' below the raised stage, while the wealthier sat in sheltered galleries or boxes. King James was a keen theatre-goer and supporter of Shakespeare's company, the King's Men, with a personal interest in witchcraft, religion and the role of the monarch. Contemporary playwrights catered for these tastes in their choice of subject matter and creation of characters.

Theatres and theatre companies

When the Globe theatre opened on the south side of the Thames in 1599, Shakespeare's company moved there from the theatre in Shoreditch which had hitherto been their home playhouse, and Shakespeare himself acquired a financial share in it. It was in the shape of a circle (which explains references in *Hamlet* and other plays performed there to globes and to the letter O), and thus offered new physical possibilities for staging. The stage was roofed but the central area was open to the sky, making lighting unnecessary since plays were performed in the afternoons. There was a trapdoor for ghosts and devils to appear from, a balcony stage above the main one, a concealed inner stage or closet, curtained off, and the projecting roof, which was referred to as 'the heavens' and may have been painted with moon and stars; Hamlet's speech in Act II scene 2 describes an 'excellent canopy…this majestical roof fretted with golden fire', and he is looking up at the roof of the Globe as he speaks.

The theatre companies of the period consisted of 12 to 14 players (doubling of parts was normal), including three or four boys to play the female roles — before their voices broke and they acquired facial hair. There were few roles for women in plays of the period, since it was unacceptable for women to perform in public, and the first female actors did not take to the stage until 1660, after the Restoration. Though they retained their own base in London, from 1600 onwards companies undertook regular tours to the provinces — sometimes unwillingly, but necessarily to boost their finances — where they performed in inns and the great halls of country houses and royal residences.

The Lord Chamberlain's Men, the company to which Shakespeare belonged as an actor and playwright, became the King's Men in 1603 on the accession of King James I. The tragedian Richard Burbage and the comedian Will Kemp were the leading actors, tragic and comic respectively, for whom Shakespeare wrote; the latter died in 1603, and there are possible allusions to his death, and the lack of a fool, in *Hamlet*.

Tragedy and the tragic hero

Tragedy originated in Dionysiac choral song in the Greece of the fifth century BC. It literally means 'goat song' (*tragoidia*), which may refer to the sacrifice of innocent creatures to propitiate the gods. In tragedy, which involves disaster and multiple deaths — some undeserved — the events seem directed by fate, which ironically overrules the intentions and desires of the human victims, creating a sense of waste when exceptional people become fallen and their qualities are lost. Tragedy is inevitable when inner values are in conflict with external circumstances. A. C. Bradley described tragedy as 'a painful mystery'.

Tragedies start with a serious early problem in the plot — related to death, war or failure of judgement — which develops into a catastrophic situation requiring further deaths and noble sacrifices in order for the previous status quo, with new participants, to be restored. During the drama there are 'incidents arousing pity and fear, wherewith to accomplish its **catharsis** of such emotions' (Aristotle, *The Poetics*). Tragedy has long been regarded as the highest **genre** of drama, having a philosophical seriousness requiring a playwright to produce work at the full stretch of his intellectual powers. At the beginning of the seventeenth century the contemporary theatrical world had a taste for tragedy. This lasted until 1606, after which more courtly, artificially structured and elaborately staged plays and masques, with spectacular effects, became fashionable.

Shakespeare's tragedies

In Shakespeare the initial conflict is caused by a mistaken decision (usually the protagonist's) based on fear or desire, taken of the person's own free will and against advice or their own better judgement. This starts off a disastrous, irreversible and seemingly inevitable chain of cause and effect, as the hero falls from high to low. Evil or irresponsible acts committed by highly placed individuals spread to involve families, court communities, and the nation, representing the contemporary belief in the connection between the **microcosm** and the **macrocosm**.

Whereas time is the healing agent in comedies, it works against the protagonists in tragedy, in the form of coincidence and urgency, aspects of a malign fate. The middle of Act III is usually the climactic scene of the conflict, and thereafter a sense of impending doom is created by the feeling that time is speeding up and out of control. There may be a **dénouement**, like the revelation of Iago's true nature to *Othello*, but more important in tragedy is the final **anagnorisis**, the recognition of a painful truth about oneself and the world. The sense of waste and loss comes from the fact that the hero has superhuman qualities in other respects and could have gone on to achieve great things. As Marlowe put it in the epilogue to *Doctor Faustus*: 'Cut is the branch that might have grown full straight.' Because free will is involved, an accident of birth or fate alone cannot be blamed, making the retribution more complex and a cause of concern to all humans, not only high-born ones.

Because high tension cannot be sustained relentlessly for more than two hours in the theatre, even in the most serious of Shakespeare's tragedies there are quasi-comic scenes, which serve as ironic juxtapositions. After the multiple body count (at least five) and restoration of justice and order, a trusted character makes the final chorus-type speech summing up the tragic events and looking forward to a brighter future; things can only get better. The audience are expected to feel purged by the extreme emotions of pity and fear they have been made to feel on another's behalf. A tragedy differs from a history play in that we are asked to identify with the hero because of his exceptional skills and virtues, and we care more about his personal sufferings than about the events of the period being represented on stage.

The major tragedies

There are striking similarities between Shakespeare's tragedies, particularly the four major ones written between 1600 and 1606, of which *Hamlet* was the first. The parallels lie not only in their plots, which are based on children and parents losing

each other; siblings, friends or couples being divorced; murders by relatives; spying and lying. Characterisation, **themes** and **imagery** also echo each other across the plays (the themes of words, appearances and poison, for example), and contradictions as well as parallels add to the complexity. For instance, Iago is an inverted image of Hamlet as the amoral instead of the moral philosopher, the latter depending on demonstrable evidence and the former disregarding it. He is also, however, a parallel to the false Claudius in *Hamlet*, who can fool others into believing him honest, who can 'smile and smile, and be a villain'.

Nature is particularly important in the major tragedies, as a main source of imagery and as the embodiment of **paradox**, being the origin of both health and disease, good and evil. In Shakespearean tragedy, uncertainty is of the essence, and fundamental human experiences and beliefs, such as love and war, are questioned and examined, but no consistent evaluation is given. Along with the tortured heroes, we have to ask ourselves: What constitutes humanity? Why are we on this earth? How can we tell right from wrong? Who is in control? We are asked for our moral awareness, but not our moral judgement, since no one is in a position to judge fellow humans, and those who believe that they are often cause the tragic situation, as in *King Lear*. Following the classical ideal, self-knowledge was the highest goal for the **Renaissance** man.

The tragic hero

The tragic hero must be someone of eminent rank within his own society, a king, prince or military leader, someone 'better than we are' (Aristotle) so that we are the more shocked by their demise. The course which each tragic hero believes will lead to success in fact leads to his destruction. In classical terms, they become guilty of **hubris**, an act of presumption as mere mortals, and their overreaching is punished by Nemesis, goddess of retribution, to which the audience are expected to respond by feeling 'the pity of it'. The 'noble hero' makes what Aristotle called an 'error of judgement' (Greek *hamartia*), which traditionally has been translated as a 'fatal (in both senses of the word) flaw'. The mistake is traceable to a character weakness, and this, in unfortunate conjunction with circumstance and coincidence, causes his awesome fall 'from happiness to misery'. During his fall he will undergo ironic and sudden reversals which bring him up against the 'realisation of the unthinkable' (C. Leech).

Shakespeare's tragic heroes

Shakespeare's major tragic heroes appear superficially to have little in common: Romeo, the immature and impetuous lover; Hamlet, the isolated, intellectual Dane; Othello, the middle-aged general and Moor, newly wed; King Lear, widower of over 80 who is losing his grip and his mind; Macbeth, the married but childless Scottish warrior and serial killer; Antony the Roman triumvir and general who gave up everything for his exotic mistress. However, they are all driven mad in one way or another, and lose touch with reason, reality and their former selves. In each case women, whether wives, daughters, mothers or witches, are a force for good or evil, and crucial to the development of the hero, the plot and the tragedy; they seem to represent nature and the extremes it is capable of. Another shared trait of the tragic male characters is their tendency to give way to passion, and thereby to extremes of behaviour. This lures them from the sobriety and safety of Aristotle's **golden mean**.

Shakespeare's heroes die **ambiguously**, either achieving a kind of dignity by showing courage in the final moments — even though possibly continuing to labour under a delusion — or passively cooperating with the workings of divine necessity. The classical view is that 'The tragic hero makes a fuss' (Leech) about what has happened to him and the injustice of the world, and dies fighting back rather than accepting the unacceptable. The other, Christian, view is that by recognising his error, taking responsibility for it, repenting of it and accepting punishment, redemption is possible for the hero. In either case, the admiration of the audience is retained or regained to the extent that we are sorry when heroes die expressing the hope that they will survive in the memory of their friends and the state, and that their true story will be told, with all its mitigating circumstances, and that something may be learned from it (such as that it is better to love wisely rather than too well).

Hamlet as tragic hero

In several ways Hamlet is an exception to the definition of a typical Shakespearean tragic hero; and it is fitting for his character that he defies the stereotype. He is royal yet has the common touch, something lacking in other tragic heroes; and perhaps most significantly, he is intentionally ironic and more intelligent, having a sharp perception and sensitive apprehension. The original sin or misjudgement was not of his making but his uncle's; he must die because of an accident of fate and not through any character defect or erroneous exercise of free will. He senses early on that he cannot win and survive, whatever choice he makes, and that a tragic outcome is inevitable. He can hardly be said to fall from high to low; rather the reverse, as he starts melancholy, burdened, and sick of this 'weary, stale, flat, and unprofitable' world, disillusioned about humans in general and his close relatives and loved ones in particular. His tragedy lies in the realisation that man cannot be a god and is perhaps no better than a beast, in the 'eternal incongruity between the divine wit and the animal grossness of man' (Lucas, p. 75). If he is tragic it is because he is an innocent victim and his death is a loss to the human race; if he is a hero it is because by the end he has redeemed himself, his parents, his country, and all humanity through his intellectual and emotional honesty, against all the odds.

Play context

It is widely assumed that Shakespeare never left England, though the majority of his plays in all **genres** are set in other countries. Italy was particularly favoured because it was the origin of the **Renaissance** and home to many of the source texts which inspired Shakespeare and his contemporaries. Foreign settings also have the advantage of allowing comments on local political and social issues to be made circumspectly, as in *Hamlet*.

Sources

Shakespeare used known **sources** for 35 of his 37 plays, and it is assumed that the other two must have had sources as yet undiscovered. In this period, before, and for some time after (until the aptly named novel in the early eighteenth century in fact), originality of plot or character was not considered necessary or even desirable in literary works. A largely illiterate population and a traditional oral culture created a demand for the familiar and reassuring, as with children and their bedtime stories. Audiences expected to already know the basic storylines, settings and outcomes of plays they attended; the skill and creativity of the playwright was demonstrated by the quality of the improvements made to an existing work, including the adaptation of the genre.

The Hamlet story is found in the folk literature of Iceland, Ireland and Denmark. It was the Danish historian Saxo Grammaticus who put it into its first literary form in a book of tragic stories printed in 1514 but written in Latin in the thirteenth century. A Hamlet play older than Shakespeare's is known to have existed, believed to have been written by Thomas Kyd as a companion piece to his *The Spanish Tragedy* (1587). Shakespeare appears to have drawn on both these for his play. A French version of the story by Belleforest was in existence, as one of his popular *Histoires tragiques*, but no translation is known of before 1608, and therefore Shakespeare must have got the story from either the original French or the 'Ur-Hamlet' of Kyd (based on the French version), in which a ghost calls out 'Hamlet, revenge' and there is a play within a play. Shakespeare's *Hamlet* is also believed to owe something to Bright's *A Treatise of Melancholy* (1586) and Florio's translation of Montaigne (June 1600) and there are similarities of style and phrasing between the soliloquies and the ironic, self-critical and conversational essays of Cornwallis circulating in 1600.

The **Trojan War**, dealt with extensively in Homer's *Iliad*, was a seminal story for succeeding generations, and the text is still being plundered today for its literary **themes**. All human experience is here: exile, nostalgia, madness, memory, betrayal, loyalty, love, war, story-telling, family, camaraderie; and, most relevantly to *Hamlet*, the power of the gods and the destruction caused by the beauty of women and men's inability to resist it.

There are three main differences between *The Spanish Tragedy* and *Hamlet*, and it is worth considering the difference of effect in each case. In the former play a father is exhorted by a ghost to avenge the murder of his son, there is a definite female suicide, and the fulfilment of revenge is delayed by purely physical impediments.

Saxo's story

In Saxo's story a king is murdered by his brother, who ascends the throne and marries the dead king's widow (Gerutha). Her son, Amleth, plans to take revenge on his uncle, and to protect himself pretends to be raving mad. The king is suspicious, and in order to find out whether the madness is genuine arranges that Amleth should be spied on by a beautiful girl. He is also spied on as he talks to his mother, and brutally kills and dismembers the court adviser who is hidden in her room. His mother promises to help him. Amleth is sent into exile in England but changes the letters to the king, and so his two companions are killed in his place. He returns in disguise after a year, gets the court drunk at a funeral feast (being held to celebrate his own supposed death), sets fire to the palace and kills his uncle after an exchange of swords. He succeeds to the throne and dies later in battle.

Shakespeare altered his source in the following ways: he added a ghost, an Ophelia figure, a Laertes figure, players and a play within a play; he introduced poison as the means of death (for Hamlet's father, Claudius, Laertes, Gertrude, and Hamlet himself) rather than simple bloodshed; and Hamlet does not stay away from Denmark a whole year, or attend his own funeral, or succeed to the throne for a significant period. Again, you should consider whether and why Shakespeare's version is an improvement.

The printed text

No manuscripts of any of Shakespeare's plays have survived. Some of the plays were published during his lifetime, in editions known as 'Quarto' from the size of the paper used. After his death, a collected edition known as the First Folio was published in 1623, which contains all his plays except *Pericles*. Although the Folio is generally considered to be more reliable than the Quartos, for each play the case has to be considered on its merits. *Hamlet* is unique in having three substantive texts: Q1 is a bad quarto, Q2 is a good quarto probably authorised by Shakespeare, and F (the Folio text) is the playhouse transcript. Although we cannot know with confidence the origins of the copies of the play, there are generally three possibilities: the author's rough draft, or 'foul papers'; a prompt copy prepared for use by a theatre; and a fair copy made by the author. Whichever it was, the text was often copied by a scribe, and then typeset in fixed metal type by a compositor, and errors or changes could creep in at any stage of this process. We know that Shakespeare often revised the texts of his plays, and often made deletions, and there is no consensus as to which is the more genuine or reliable text. Since he rarely provided localities or stage directions, much has been left to the discretion of editors through the ages.

For any Shakespeare play three dates must be considered: the completion of the manuscript, the first performance and the first printing. The added complexity in the case of *Hamlet* is that there are also three distinct texts.

The title page of the First Quarto, printed in 1603, reads: *The Tragical History of Hamlet, Prince of Denmark,* advertised as having been 'diverse times acted by his Highness' servants'. This version is shorter than the one now generally used; the philosophical speeches are truncated and it is probably a pirated version taken from a stage performance, containing many errors. The names of some of the characters are different from the other versions, including that of Polonius (Corambis). Some scholars believe that it is a corrupt text reconstructed from memory by the actor who played Marcellus; others think that it may have been a reconstruction by a small touring company (like the players in *Hamlet*) who wanted to perform an abridged version. Though generally dismissed as an unauthorised text, editors and directors sometimes make use of Q1 as a witness to early performances and incorporate its stage directions, such as having the Ghost appear in Gertrude's closet 'in his night gown' or mad Ophelia 'playing on a lute, and her hair down singing'.

Q2, which appeared in 1604 or 1605, is nearly twice as long as Q1 and, unlike its predecessor, was probably published with Shakespeare's approval, since it claims on its title page to be 'the true and perfect copy', which meant that it had accessed the playwright's original manuscript or 'foul papers'. This version is characterised by the casualness of its character numbering, with frequent references to 'a man or two' and 'all the rest'. Q2 forms the basis of the accepted text of Hamlet, Q3 not being sufficiently different to merit attention. Q2 does, however, lack some of the famous passages of F's dialogue, and substantively differs from F in 36% of its printed lines, with 88 lines in F having no counterpart in Q2 and 222 lines in Q2 with no counterpart in F.

The Folio edition, compiled seven years after the playwright's death, was the work of fellow actors who had access to the company's playbooks, including the prompter's annotations. It therefore has more stage directions but omits 230 lines from some of the longer and more philosophical passages, as befits a text meant more as an acting than a reading version, with a concern for the pace of the performance. A full-text conflation of Q2 and Folio, the basis for most current editions of the text, would take four hours in performance and is therefore normally cut significantly by directors. The Folio enables editors to correct misprints and restore the passages omitted from Q2, so a modern edition of Hamlet will be based on Q2 but make some use of F, the traditionally favoured reading.

There are significant differences between the two texts in individual word choices, some of which would be of interest to an A-level student. Any decent edition will have notes in which editors explain the **cruces** and justify their preferred reading. The latest Arden edition (ed. Taylor and Thompson, 2006) and the revised Penguin Shakespeare (ed. T. J. B. Spencer, 2005) are principally based upon the second Quarto, but include additions from F. They disagree on details, which can subtly alter the interpretation of character or **imagery**, for example whether Laertes says 'Thus didest thou' or 'Thus diest thou' (Act IV scene 7) or whether Hamlet's first **soliloquy** uses the adjective 'sullied' or 'solid' before 'flesh' in the first line. Examiners are aware that no two published texts of *Hamlet* are identical and will either accept quotations from whichever edition you are using, or expect you to use the edition the board has prescribed.

Whichever edition you use, a number of changes will have been made from the original text, and different editors often have different views and arrive at different conclusions. The changes and arguments for them are usually indicated in the textual notes. Generally, the goal of an editor is to produce an edition that makes sense when acted on the stage, rather than to give an account of all the possible interpretations of the play.

Verse and prose

Verse tended to be given to noble and royal characters, expressing romantic or elevated feelings, and at certain heightened moments they use **rhyming couplets**. These are also used at the ends of scenes to give them an air of finality — often sinister — or for spells, songs or some other special form of utterance. Couplets also suggest that common wisdom is being quoted, or a more archaic form is being used, as in the *Murder of Gonzago* passages within *Hamlet*. Prose was generally reserved for characters of lower social status, for comic or domestic scenes, or to indicate secrecy or conspiracy; Hamlet switches backwards and forwards between verse and prose, and the play is unusual for Shakespeare in being 27% prose.

It is always significant and needs to be interpreted if a character who normally uses verse switches to prose, and vice versa. Characters who suddenly become less fluent, articulate or capable of speaking in a smooth rhythm are often undergoing emotional disturbance or rapid thinking, for example:

LAERTES: He is justly served.
    It is a poison tempered by himself.
    Exchange forgiveness with me, noble Hamlet.
    Mine and my father's death come not upon thee,
    Nor thine on me!

Students should be aware of the prose sequences in the play and the effect created by their contrast with what precedes and follows in each case. They also need to note which characters rarely use or are uncomfortable with prose, such as Claudius,

whose metrical regularity rarely falters, and those who change according to their **interlocutor** or context, like Ophelia, a passive pawn pushed between the men of the play, who does not seem to have a voice of her own. Hamlet shows his contempt for, rather than intimacy with, several of the other characters by talking to them in prose (using the excuse of his supposed madness), whereas he speaks verse to Horatio and Gertrude.

There are different types of prose, in terms of register and complexity of syntax, and this plays a role in the delineation of character and is an indicator of the state of a relationship. A formal register used in an informal situation, such as Hamlet uses to Rosencrantz and Guildenstern in Act III scene 2, conveys sarcasm. **Colloquial** diction in a public setting is equally odd and in need of comment, as when Hamlet addresses the Ghost as 'old mole' (I.5.162). 'You' is either a plural or an indication of respect to someone of higher authority, whereas 'thou', the singular form, suggests familiarity or affection, or talking down to a social inferior. This meant that it could be used as an insult or to suggest an irregular intimacy, and, conversely, using 'you' to a family member would convey coldness and a hostile relationship, as in Claudius's address to his stepson, compared to his mother's.

Despite his anguish, Hamlet is never reduced to monosyllables or repetition, unlike Othello for instance, and is always articulate, but he uses a variety of registers in both verse and prose, even in **soliloquies**, which should be noted and interpreted.

The play on stage

Hamlet, the first of Shakespeare's major tragedies, was popular from its first performance in 1601. It has been in continual production for 400 years, and is the most often performed of Shakespeare's plays. This was true even by 1710, when Shaftesbury described it as the play 'most to have affected English hearts'. More than any other of Shakespeare's works it has become a global phenomenon and for many people it is the title most synonymous with its author. The play has become part of the collective unconscious of the Western world, and perhaps even further afield.

Although performed according to an infinite variety of settings and stagings, there is little scope, compared to other tragedies, for altering the basic presentation of the characters. Polonius can be made more or less ridiculous, and Rosencrantz and Guildenstern more or less naive, but Claudius is always duplicitous, Laertes is always misguided, Horatio is always worthy. The women have been treated to a wider range of approaches, from devious to pathetic, but antipathy towards Claudius and sympathy towards Hamlet have been conveyed by the vast majority of directors (though not by all critics), which makes it different from *Othello* and *King Lear*, in which the main parts have been variously interpreted to the extent of the heroes and villains swapping roles. Changes of emphasis have rather been provided by setting the play in particular countries, periods and political contexts, and by the judicious cutting of lines or repositioning of speeches; the 'To be' **soliloquy** has often been positioned before the arrival of the Players rather than after.

Because it has all been done before, the challenge nowadays to come up with a novel production of *Hamlet* drives directors to become ever more outrageous; one recent production used scooters and helicopters. Though this can be irritating (and distracts from the language) it makes the point that this is a play for all times, and Hamlet is a man for all seasons. The director Janet Suzman wrote in the programme of her South African-based production of May 2006 at Stratford's Swan Theatre:

> Hamlet is first detained under house arrest, then banished, then under order of execution. His so-called friends spy and report on him. He is in physical danger in a state run by a tyrant…There are many countries in the world which still fit this description today, and they are not fictional.

As Shakespeare's longest play by far, it would take about four hours to perform in full, even if the lines were spoken fast, and it is almost always cut in production; the play was heavily cut during its initial performance period, losing up to 800 lines. Some scenes or passages have been routinely cut, such as the prologue to the Mousetrap, and for much of the play's history the closet scene ended at Act III scene 4, line 179 ('I must be cruel only to be kind'), in order to avoid the sexual description (but also cutting out Gertrude's avowal of loyalty to Hamlet). Major plot elements such as Ophelia's funeral and the Laertes–Claudius sub-plot have been 'taken to the barber' to reduce the running time of the performance. Remarkably, Fortinbras was usually absent until the very late nineteenth century, much to Shaw's disgust. Nineteenth-century productions usually ended with Hamlet's last words, but this ignores the tragic imperative to ensure an appropriate succession and future for the state, and for the new ruler or remaining figure of highest authority to make a speech summing up the action and commenting on the dead hero. Although the play is long, because the scenes start *in medias res* and are full of interruptions, entrances and exits, the pace seems fast and counteracts the early absence of action and the dilatory effect of the seven soliloquies.

The Ghost

The presentation of the Ghost and its effect on Hamlet offers the greatest scope for not only special effects but also variant interpretations; traditionally it is believed that Shakespeare himself delighted in playing the part of the Ghost. Until the nineteenth century Hamlets took the manifestation manfully, but since then every possible physical and emotional response has been tried. The actual staging of the Ghost is a perennial problem: a realistic character dressed as a ghost; a suggestion of a physical supernatural presence; a voice only? If there is no visible ghost, the **gothic** horror of the compelling opening scene is lost, as is the redolent **imagery** of a dead man in full armour walking the battlements. On the other hand, what can only be heard but not seen is always more frightening. Tastes change in theatre as in everything else: the Ghost has been dressed in armour, a nightgown, all in white, all in black, and as a host of other permutations of the animate and inanimate, natural and supernatural. Films, of course, have the advantage over theatre of being able to digitally enhance their effects, as can be seen in Branagh's version (1996), which emphasises the territorial war and power struggle between Denmark and Norway by using a giant statue of old Hamlet to represent the Ghost, which is destroyed in the final sequence by the invading Norwegians.

Hamlets

The role of Hamlet was created for and originally played by Richard Burbage (1568–1619), England's first celebrated tragic actor. Actors made the part their own for remarkably long periods, with Thomas Betterton, for instance, playing it until he was 74 (1661 to 1709). Because of this longevity of their performances, actors added 'points' to personalise their interpretation and make it distinctive and memorable, such as the crawling introduced into the Mousetrap scene by Edmund Kean in 1814. 'Angels and ministers of grace defend us!' (I.4.39) became a spectacular line for Garrick because of his raised hands and his wearing of a wig which stood its hair on end at this point.

Hamlets are either vigorous or sentimental; he was played as a manly character in the seventeenth century, in contrast with the sensitive melancholic of the late eighteenth and early nineteenth centuries, an interpretation David Garrick (1717–79) gave to the role for 34 years from 1742. John Kemble introduced a more sorrowful, wistful prince in his performance of the role between 1783 and 1817, contemporaneously with the first female Hamlet, his sister Sarah Siddons, who played it for 30 years from 1776. There is a long tradition of female Hamlets, the most celebrated being Sarah Bernhardt, who first played the part in 1899. The American actor Edwin Booth, who performed the role from 1853 to 1891, was apparently haunted by the ghost of his father, who had himself played Hamlet for 20 years. There is a tradition of the Ghost being played by an actor who has previously played Hamlet. Even in the twentieth century Gielgud played the part occasionally between 1929 and 1945, a time span unheard of in the modern theatre.

Because Hamlet speaks so many of the lines and is on stage for so many of the scenes, the part is more demanding than that of Othello or even King Lear. Since he must feign madness, adopt different speech modes and moods, and engage in strenuous physical activity, it is a young man's role. However, there is a problem with determining Hamlet's age, and therefore with the casting of the part. He is 30 according to the text in Act V scene 1, but given that his mother is still apparently sprightly and attractive, it is unlikely that she could have been as old as 44, at least (allowing for the fact that noblewomen married at 14) at a time when this would be considered extreme old age. (Although it would explain Hamlet's admonition in Act III scene 4 that at her age she should no longer be interested in sex.) She is usually played, however, as someone young and sexy enough to be considered as at least a possible fixation for an **Oedipus complex**, as well as an object of desire to Claudius, which is not consistent with her being a matronly figure. In practice, both she and Hamlet are usually played by actors considerably younger, which supports the 'rebellious teenager' interpretation of Hamlet's behaviour that accords with modern expectations of an adolescent. However, by the end of the play he seems considerably more mature, and it is not implausible that he could be in his late twenties and still a student. The older he is, the more explicable would be his disappointment that Claudius has 'popped between the election and [his] hopes' of succeeding his father.

As a Dane, Hamlet is traditionally assumed to be blond (hence the Olivier and Branagh peroxide portrayals), but there is nothing in the text that demands this, and it could be said to go against the melancholy and black-suited aspects of the character. Other decisions a director has to make are whether Hamlet's relationship with his mother is unnaturally close; whether his distaste for female sexuality has reached the point of homosexuality (he has been played by some famous homosexuals, such as Laurence Olivier and Derek Jacobi); whether to stage rather than report the Ophelia closet scene; whether to make the relationship between Claudius and Gertrude physically explicit; how much of a buffoon to make Polonius; and how flirtatious and complicit to make Ophelia (in Branagh's film, Kate Winslet is a consenting partner in a full sexual relationship with Hamlet). A more mundane dilemma is where to place the interval, which would usually fall at the end of Act III, but in this play Act IV scene 1 is clearly a continuation of the action; the influence of early editors means an act break, often observed as the interval, is usually put in the middle of the closet scene.

Staging through the ages

Plays started at 2 p.m., hence the stress at the beginning of the play on it being midnight and very dark: language had to do here what lighting could not, since there wasn't any. There were also no sets to speak of, or detailed stage directions: just actors and the text. In the eighteenth century the play regularly toured the provinces, and scenery was then introduced. From the late nineteenth century onwards the actor–manager figure gave way to the director, who experimented with interpretation and ruled over the production.

Originally the lines would have been delivered naturalistically, as Hamlet himself would have wished. By the eighteenth century, however, people went to the theatre to see and be seen, and the play on stage was incidental to the social event. Theatrical language, with its town-crier-like exaggerations full of **rhetorical** flourishes, became as artificial as the dress of the theatre-goers. Such a declamatory style of acting was necessary to keep the audience's attention and combat distraction in the crowded and noisy theatre, where people chatted freely in their boxes. In this period actors made a part their own and attracted an audience through their own fame and personality rather than for the merit of the play. At the end of the seventeenth century 816 lines had been cut from the play, which ended with the last exit of Ophelia; Garrick replaced 629 of them, but did not fully restore Act V, which ended 60 lines before the end of Shakespeare's text and without Fortinbras. All 'absurd digressions' and anything 'disgusting' was removed by Garrick, which seriously reduced the roles of the two women. He excised the gravedigger scene in a 1772 production on the grounds that it was 'an indecorous intrusion of the low, mean and detestable upon the sublime and the great'. This century disapproved of bawdiness, the mingling of **genres**, and failure to dispense **poetic justice** in accordance with the demands of neoclassicism, to the extent that *King Lear* and other tragedies were given comedy endings!

The nineteenth century saw a switch of focus from hearing to reading the text. Shakespeare was Keats's 'presiding genius' and he was not alone in preferring to enjoy the bard as a solitary occupation. Shakespeare became a literary icon in the Romantic period and the word 'bardolatry' was coined to express the reverence for the great playwright, whose plays were mined for their worship of nature and celebration of the imagination. The characters became subjects of paintings, most famously Ophelia. Sir Henry Irving was the most important actor of the lead role in this century. His Hamlet was more reflective and langorous than Garrick's, less rhetorical and more natural. Throughout this century the role of Gertrude continued to be cut, with the effect of eliminating the possibility of her being viewed as sympathetic in the closet scene.

In the twentieth century, productions of *Hamlet* started to have design values to aid interpretation, and sets became important. A bed was added to the set of the closet scene for the first time, which inevitably introduced Freudian psychology and the shade of Oedipus. In the 1989 Royal Shakespeare Company (RSC) production directed by Ron Daniels, the 'wonky window' backdrop subsiding from left to right reflected the **theme** of falling and Denmark being 'out of joint'. Mark Rylance (until recently artistic director of the Globe) played Hamlet as a rebel and outsider, delivering his first **soliloquy** with his back to the audience and wearing pyjamas. He conveyed a prince who was not at all sweet and who was genuinely mad, aggressive and nasty. In 1997 Alex Jennings played the title role in a much cut and altered version of the play, in which the Ghost appeared at the wedding reception for his widow and his brother. There was no Fortinbras, again, and the production was centred upon family rather then political discord, with a bulimic Ophelia.

The next century continued the concept of the nasty Hamlet with the 2001 RSC production with Sam West, whom audiences were not supposed to like. The set consisted of CCTV cameras to convey the spying theme, and lots of cold, empty, loveless space. Hamlet's feelings towards his mother were definitely aggression rather than desire. Modern productions cannot escape expectations foisted upon them by audience experience of cinema. As the director Janet Suzman said of her 2006 Stratford production of *Hamlet*: 'Casting is 90% of your view of a play.' A play which is being acted somewhere in the world all the time can only be renewed by a choice of a different character to play Hamlet, which dictates the flavour of the entire production. All Hamlets journey into the darkness in search of some illumination, but that is all they have in common. As the introduction to the Penguin edition says, 'Hamlets have come in all shapes and sizes since Burbage' and the text demands of the actor 'a combination of any number of qualities: stamina, vulnerability, charm, lunacy, wit, anger, vocal technique and variety, arrogance, melancholy, classicism, **colloquialism**, **irony**, generosity and cruelty' (p. lxx). Each director and/or actor will choose to emphasise one of these qualities over the others, thus producing a new Hamlet each time.

Critical history

This is the most discussed play in the world, and at any time it is being performed and reviewed somewhere. In recent years the number of critical publications has been over 400 a year. What has been referred to as the 'megagigantic body of commentary on *Hamlet*' was forecast by its earliest reception. According to the Allusion Book (first published in 1874, listing all references to Shakespeare between 1591 and 1700), *Hamlet* was Shakespeare's most popular play in the seventeenth century. Speculation about what the enigmatic hero means when he says that he has 'that within which passes show' (I.2.85) has teased critics for centuries. A fixture on exam specifications, *Hamlet* is deemed to be an accessible text for students because it has universal appeal and because the hero is considered a more empathic character for teenagers than the other tragic heroes — largely because he has a sense of humour, shares his thoughts with the audience, and has problems easily identified with: a dysfunctional family and disappointment in love and friendship.

Nineteenth-century criticism

The first generation of critics, in the eighteenth century, were overly concerned about the sexual and religious morality of the play — Dr Johnson admitted to being revolted by Hamlet's reasons for not killing Claudius while praying. So Shakespeare's genius and the achievement of the tragedies were not fully appreciated until the beginning of the Romantic period, towards the end of the century, when analysis of psychological states and human relationships became the focus of critical interest. Hamlet was perceived as an abstract of **Everyman** and a **symbolic** political figure in an age of revolutions, the paralysed liberal incapable of necessary action. The Romantics could also identify with Hamlet because of his melancholy and madness,

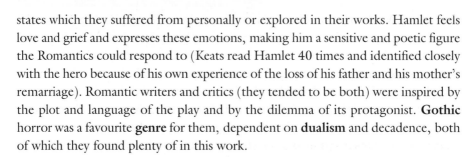

states which they suffered from personally or explored in their works. Hamlet feels love and grief and expresses these emotions, making him a sensitive and poetic figure the Romantics could respond to (Keats read Hamlet 40 times and identified closely with the hero because of his own experience of the loss of his father and his mother's remarriage). Romantic writers and critics (they tended to be both) were inspired by the plot and language of the play and by the dilemma of its protagonist. **Gothic** horror was a favourite **genre** for them, dependent on **dualism** and decadence, both of which they found plenty of in this work.

Samuel Taylor Coleridge was the important critic at the turn of the century who responded intuitively and appreciatively to the emotions being explored through the medium of the main characters. He argued influentially that Hamlet was prevented from acting because he thought too much and 'lost the power of action in the energy of resolve'. Coleridge saw Hamlet as a psychological study of a man who could not achieve a balance between his inward thoughts and the external world, describing him as an introvert with a 'proportionate aversion to real action' (Jump p. 30). The Romantic critics generally, and their successors, saw the delay as inextricably bound up with, and a manifestation of, the hero's character. The play's women were treated with more respect but also more **pathos** than hitherto. By the time of the Pre-Raphaelite movement in art, the much-used motif of poets and novelists of associating women with water (and thereby a passive death) was employed in portrayals of Ophelia's drowning; Millais depicted her as floating dead and horizontal (1852), whereas earlier artistic depictions had stressed her upright, tree-climbing aspect.

The play remained popular throughout the nineteenth century, with Hamlet's procrastination and relationship with his mother the main issues for literary debate. Leading critics towards the end of the period became much exercised over whether Hamlet is actually mad or only feigns madness, prompting Oscar Wilde to ask wittily 'Are Hamlet's critics mad, or only pretending to be so?'

Twentieth-century criticism

By the beginning of the next century the novel had become the dominant literary form, which encouraged critics to focus on the character of the hero of *Hamlet*, and to disagree about it. They were not, however, generally very kind to him. Sigmund Freud was influenced by the play when formulating his theory of the **Oedipus complex** (first published in *The Interpretation of Dreams*, 1900) and for psychoanalytical critics Hamlet and Ophelia became icons of male and female neurosis. There have since been a myriad of interpretations of his state of mind, most of them incompatible. Thus began the tendency for critics to see Hamlet as suffering from their own fears and weaknesses, and to attribute to him their own pet theories, as claimed by C. S. Lewis, whose own pet theory was that Hamlet is not an individual at all, but **Everyman**, haunted by original sin and fear of death. Some were certainly extreme, such as that Hamlet is suffering from obesity, that he is actually the son of Claudius, that he is jealous of the foetus the pregnant Gertrude is carrying, and, inevitably, that he is homosexual. T. S. Eliot used Hamlet in his 1920 essays on poetry and criticism as an example of his theory of the need for art to have an **'objective correlative'**, and accused Hamlet of displaying emotion 'in excess of the facts as they appear' at the beginning of the play, arguing that this made *Hamlet* a failure as a work of art. A. C. Bradley, on the other hand, stressed the fact that Hamlet had sustained a paralysing shock as a result of his mother's second marriage and that he was suffering from clinical melancholia (not to be confused with insanity), his whole mind having been poisoned by what he has discovered about his nearest and dearest, particularly the females, and his pain being the more intense for his being a highly imaginative person. G. B. Shaw and Middleton Murray ascribed Hamlet's delay to his Christian belief and a moral repugnance towards the concept of revenge, since only self-defence could justify breaking one of the ten commandments. Freud's biographer, Ernest Jones, in 'Hamlet Psychoanalysed' (1949), famously diagnosed Hamlet as a 'tortured conscience' suffering from an Oedipus complex, whereby a son's interest in his mother has sexual overtones. According to his Freudian interpretation, Hamlet's failure to act is due to his repressed jealousy of his father and desire for his mother, which inner conflict paralyses him since to kill his father substitute would be admitting to incestuous feelings.

The most hostile twentieth-century critics claimed that Hamlet is essentially an egotist who has no intention of avenging his father's death, and in the end avenges only his own. Shaw thought it was absolutely clear that Hamlet the intellectual is not interested in revenge, or even in being King of Denmark, and except when excited does not feel motivated to kill anyone; as he graphically puts it: 'revenge is not worth the mess the king's blood would make on the floor.' G. Wilson Knight (1930) argues in favour of Claudius, claiming that he is more human than Hamlet, who has seen through humanity and become cynical, and that all the other characters in the play ally themselves with Claudius and are all leagued against Hamlet because they are puzzled by and fear him. Hamlet is allegedly the poison in the healthy bustle of court life, 'an element of evil in the state of Denmark', and the Ghost is the devil of knowledge and death, using Hamlet to spread hell on earth. C. S. Lewis said in 1942 that he would not cross the room to meet Hamlet because he is a man 'incapable of achievement because of his inability to understand either himself or his fellows or the real quality of the universe which has produced him'. He also argued that attention to Hamlet's character misses the real point of the play, which is the mystery of human existence. In 1950 E. M. W. Tillyard included *Hamlet* in his book entitled *Shakespeare's Problem Plays*. Feminist critics, such as Elaine Showalter, saw Ophelia as a female archetype of the schizophrenic suffering from the malady of repressed sexuality

(as opposed to the male archetype of insanity, 'the mad professor', whose problem is over-intelligence). Hamlet has not emerged any more unscathed from the feminist critique than from the psychoanalytical one, which is not surprising, given the attitudes he expresses towards Gertrude and Ophelia in the play and the pressures he submits them to. Patricia Barnard attracted some support for her claim that Hamlet impregnates Ophelia then abandons her, and this leads to her committing suicide, so he is her murderer on two counts.

As can be seen from the above critical positions, this play has suffered more than most from critics selecting evidence that supports a particular critique or interpretation and ignoring passages of equal importance that do not. Examples include the claim that Claudius and Fortinbras are secretly in league (explained by their having a common enemy in old/young Hamlet and their political ambitiousness) and that it is therefore for Claudius, not Hamlet, that Fortinbras orders a state funeral at the end. Some critics have totally dismissed Hamlet's positive qualities, and some his defects; many have gone so far as to deny the evidence of the text in order to condemn or rehabilitate him in accordance with their own moral views. Political as well as personal opinion has influenced responses to the play, and Hamlet has been called a democrat, a communist, a revolutionary and a conservative — truly a man who is all things to all people and whom everyone can identify with.

Delay and taintedness?

The critics have always fallen into two main groups: those who assert that Hamlet did not delay in carrying out the task, and a larger group insisting that he did, and offering different explanations for his procrastination. The point is that a play that shifts its ground and sends up smoke screens invites such inconclusive readings, which is what the play is trying to prove: the truth is hard to dig out. To the present day, critics are divided over the extent to which they consider Hamlet admirable or culpable in not leaping to do his father's ghost's bidding — or whether he should have listened to the Ghost at all — and over his real reason for deferring revenge in the prayer scene. The idea of the irresolute prince has dominated discussion in recent years and given a platform to the supporters of the psychoanalytical critique. The indecisiveness of Hamlet has been stressed either to highlight a character weakness or to suggest that his dilemma is insoluble. Commentators have often overlooked the fact that from the end of Act III (and his killing of Polonius) onwards, Hamlet could be said to have become very resolute indeed, no longer questioning or arguing against the dictates of his fate. They have also often disallowed the necessity for an educated, reflective person (and future king) to act responsibly, which includes checking the sources and testing the veracity of information he is given. The twenty-first century is tired of the delay question and it is unfashionable to put all the emphasis of an interpretation of the play on this issue, which is now considered exhausted or irrelevant. The axiom 'No delay, no play' is enough of an explanation for modern-day critics, and should perhaps be enough for modern-day students.

A related cause of critical dissent concerns to what extent, if any, Hamlet becomes corrupted himself, whether or not he is able to obey his father's injunction to 'Taint not thy mind'. If he is infected by the rottenness of Denmark, then we have the **paradox** of a wicked man being used as an agent of divine providence to punish greater wickedness, and of a hero who has become disillusioned, cynical and jaded. It is true that his decision to give up 'thinking too precisely on th'event' is horribly similar to Macbeth's decision to give up thinking and just do what he feels like doing; but it can be argued that Hamlet does not embrace butchery, or use others to do his dirty work for him, and that he does retain his lofty perch above the rest of mankind, especially those who have succumbed to base urges. He keeps faith with his father's memory and command, commits no evil act intentionally, deals death only where it is due, and resists the temptation to be cruel to his mother. Hamlet is corrupt only in being a fallen human, but he does not further degrade the race; his self-admonitions are undeserved to an ironic degree, and he never departs from his own high standard of justice. His verbal scourging of the other characters can in every case be argued as being deserved, even Ophelia's. She does not have to report him to her father, and other Shakespeare heroines would not have done so. She has made her choice between the two men and must live, or die, by it. It must be admitted, however, that Hamlet is not exactly successful: Denmark has fallen into the hands of a foreigner and he has been directly or indirectly responsible for the deaths of seven people, including his mother — eight including himself.

A variety of critiques

Any play must be considered in relation to its historical and social background and the political climate which produced it, and be viewed in the context of contemporary attitudes, however unconsciously drawn on. On the other hand, our critical interpretations should include responses to the issues which concern us nowadays, such as the stereotyping of gender in the portrayal of women. A feminist critique will try to ascertain whether the play challenges or accepts and endorses the patriarchal status quo and the misogyny of the time; a psychoanalytical analysis will focus on Hamlet's isolation, sanity, indecisiveness, mood shifts and unstable ego, and glorification of his dead father; a structuralist approach will look at language and philosophy to expose the shifting and ambivalent relationship between words and meaning (signifier and signified); post-structuralists will look for what isn't there as well as what is, at how the plot is framed and at the assumptions being made. A combination of all of these critical approaches will produce essays that show an awareness of a range of reader responses and audience reactions, and that cover all the examination assessment criteria.

Scene summaries and notes

Act I scene 1

> The ghost of Hamlet's recently dead father, the late King of Denmark, appears to soldiers on watch and Hamlet's friend Horatio on the ramparts of Elsinore castle for the third time. They decide to tell Hamlet.

The play fittingly starts in a gothic setting of midnight (the clock has just struck) on castle walls in mid-winter, with insecurity and suspicion caused by the war footing Denmark is secretly on, the difficulty in recognising friend from foe, and the previous sightings of an armed ghostly figure. The half lines reveal a jumpiness and tense atmosphere; the soldiers refuse to name the Ghost, but call it a 'thing' (l. 21). The dialogue begins significantly with a question, and one which carries resonance beyond the simple enquiry to reverberate throughout the play: who is there, watching and controlling humanity? Questions continue to be asked throughout this scene. The two soldiers on watch establish the pattern of similar or contrasting pairs of characters. Horatio plays the part of the stoic and sceptic – a foil throughout the play to the mercurial Hamlet – which makes it all the more convincing when the Ghost does appear. In contrast to the setting of darkness and death, the waiting of the watch for the appearance of the Ghost is reminiscent of the shepherds waiting for the star to appear and reacting with fear and wonder. Three is the magical and mystical number, and the fact that it appeared the previous two nights makes the audience certain that it will again. When it does, it interrupts the story Barnardo is telling, the first of many interruptions in the play: death is an interruption to the tale of one's life. When Horatio the scholar is implored to speak to it by the soldiers, because their weapons are ineffectual, the play's dichotomy between words and swords, and the question of their relative strengths, is introduced. The Ghost's refusal to speak on this occasion delays the moment of revelation, delay being another recurring device and **theme** of the play. The 'strange eruption' microcosmically connects the diseased human body with the rotten state, and the 'sweaty haste' of line 77 is suggestive of sex as well as war. Horatio narrates the heroic story (and will be given this role again at the end of the play) of the vanquishing of Old Fortinbras by Old Hamlet, establishing the rivalry between the neighbouring countries, which is the framework plot to the action of this play, and introducing the motif of duels as well as the pair of dead fathers. Eyes and watching and theatre diction (such as 'prologue', l. 123) are referred to several times in this opening scene, the first of many in which characters observe and play the passive role of audience and witness to a dramatic and unnatural event. Heaven and earth are linked (l. 124) immediately prior to an eruption from hellish purgatory, the third and lowest level, the 'womb of earth' (l. 138). The crowing cock is not only an interruption and deflection, being a herald of daybreak (the time at which all spirits must return to their dark and earthy 'confine'), but is associated with the betrayal of Christ and contrasts with the wholesome image of Christmas in the speech by Marcellus which follows. The duel between dark and light, good and evil, has been declared, and 'young Hamlet', first mentioned only in line 171 at the end of the scene, is introduced into this cosmic battle context.

Act I scene 2

King Claudius, brother of the previous king and new husband to his widow, dispatches ambassadors to Norway to avert invasion. Laertes is granted permission to resume his martial arts in Paris, but Hamlet is refused permission to return to his intellectual studies in Wittenberg, and criticised by both Claudius and his mother for protracted mourning for his father, though he is only recently dead. When alone Hamlet expresses disgust at his mother's 'o'erhasty' and, as he sees it, 'incestuous' remarriage. When informed of the existence of the Ghost, Hamlet agrees to join the watch that night.

It is typical of Claudius to put on a show with trumpet and procession, to take centre stage, and to speak at length in an elevated manner using the royal plural. He performs feats of political diplomacy and personal manipulation in front of a full audience, using external threat to distract attention from domestic problems. He insistently refers to the blood ties of brother and sister and son to reassure the court that the family is secure and he the head of it. His marriage to Gertrude, whom he refers to as 'Th'imperial jointress to this warlike state' (l. 9) consolidates and seems to legitimise his usurped position (though the Queen's voice would normally be given to her son on the death of the father, if he were old enough, and she traditionally should have spent a legal term of 40 days as a dowager). He ingratiates himself with Polonius and Laertes by praising them. One of the characteristics of Claudius's speech, which intimates his insincerity, is the over-use of the name of his **interlocutor** to flatter them that they have his full attention; his unnecessary repetition of Laertes's name in particular prepares the audience for his future manipulation of him. The editor of the Arden edition points out that Laertes, with his name stressed four times in nine lines, is also being spotlighted as Hamlet's foil and foe, and 'young Fortinbras', also nephew to a king, is presented as another parallel to 'young Hamlet'.

Though he seems efficient, imposing and confident, Claudius's speeches contain repetition, digression and contortion of syntax, all denoting duplicity. He is putting on an act, which Hamlet can see through, and the duel between 'mighty opposites' begins. This is the first of the three ceremonial court scenes in which Hamlet and Claudius come face to face; they always meet in public, and always with mutual hostility barely concealed. They use the formal 'you' to each other, showing there is no love lost despite their close blood relationship. Ernest Jones has pointed out that Hamlet's malaise predates his discovery of the knowledge of the murder of his father, and therefore stems from his problematic relationship with and disappointment with his mother, whom he suspects of having betrayed his father and himself out of lust, and a pre-existing dislike of his uncle. Hamlet is not appeased by being named Claudius's successor. The **imagery** of mouths, stomachs and

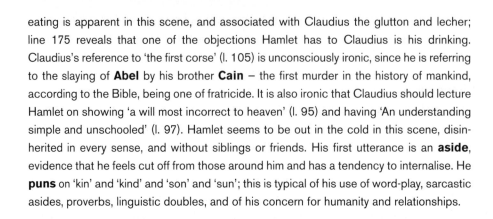

eating is apparent in this scene, and associated with Claudius the glutton and lecher; line 175 reveals that one of the objections Hamlet has to Claudius is his drinking. Claudius's reference to 'the first corse' (l. 105) is unconsciously ironic, since he is referring to the slaying of **Abel** by his brother **Cain** – the first murder in the history of mankind, according to the Bible, being one of fratricide. It is also ironic that Claudius should lecture Hamlet on showing 'a will most incorrect to heaven' (l. 95) and having 'An understanding simple and unschooled' (l. 97). Hamlet seems to be out in the cold in this scene, disinherited in every sense, and without siblings or friends. His first utterance is an **aside**, evidence that he feels cut off from those around him and has a tendency to internalise. He **puns** on 'kin' and 'kind' and 'son' and 'sun'; this is typical of his use of word-play, sarcastic asides, proverbs, linguistic doubles, and of his concern for humanity and relationships.

Act I scene 3

Laertes, about to set off for Paris, warns his sister Ophelia against losing her virginity to Hamlet, and his father Polonius forbids the relationship entirely.

Though necessary to establish the other family at court, the placement of this scene also has the effect of delaying the plot and creating suspense for the audience. Here we meet another father-and-son pair, and the love interest connecting the two families. Though a modern audience finds Polonius's maxims of worldly prudence sententious and tedious, a contemporary audience would have respected him, as his children appear to do, as a devoted father and loyal courtier, bearing in mind that his topics – speech, deportment, clothing and so on – were regular paternal and social concerns of the time. There is no **irony** (and Laertes evinces none elsewhere) in the line 'A double blessing is a double grace' (l. 53), although Laertes is returning to Paris, not setting off for the first time, so this could be a double double blessing. Polonius's platitudes actually serve to introduce many of Hamlet's concerns, such as not giving 'any unproportioned thought his act' (l. 60), and the themes of truth, memory and appearance versus reality. We learn later on that Gertrude would have welcomed Ophelia as a daughter-in-law, so this is the first of several examples of Polonius's misjudgement and lack of perception, though his motives may be unobjectionable and his attitude to his daughter standard for the period. A further irony is that while he regards Ophelia as naive and foolish, her instincts are sound about Hamlet, whom she believes to have declared love to her 'In honourable fashion' (l. 111). The descriptions of Hamlet's behaviour here, and his love poetry, imply a more youthful Hamlet than the 30-year-old of the graveyard scene. Polonius is a word-player like Hamlet, though a very inferior and laboured one, and vies with him for the role of court jester. He often takes up a word and repeats it in another sense, as he does in this scene with 'tender' and 'fashion'. Laertes is his father's son in his predilection for long, derivative speeches.

Act I scene 4

The Ghost appears and beckons Hamlet away from his companions.

This scene, itself a duplication of the first scene and using the same delaying tactics to increase suspense, gives an opportunity for Hamlet to express his views on custom, honour, evil, and defective humanity. Hamlet characteristically catechises the Ghost, as he did with Horatio at the end of scene 2. Horatio may well put the idea of feigning madness into Hamlet's mind in line 74, reminding him that this was a common response to unbearable grief (as Ophelia later illustrates). Hamlet's first response to the apparition is to recognise 'My fate cries out' (l. 81), a recognition which becomes obscured and deferred but to which he returns in Act V, having been shown the truth of Horatio's concluding line in this scene: 'Heaven will direct it.' There is ironic juxtaposition of the old and new kings and their present situation with the reference to the revelry going on in the background. This speech was cut in Q1 and F, perhaps not to give offence to James I's Danish queen, but it prolongs the suspense to include it in full and gives the Ghost's appearance the dramatic effect of an interruption. The walking of the Ghost represents forces of unreason and chaos in an unquiet Denmark. He has been put into the confines of his grave and it is a breakdown of the natural order that he should climb out of it again. He is a figure who moves physically and conceptually between the layers of earth, hell and heaven. Hamlet thinks of his late father as a divine being above mere mortals, a 'goodly king' and great soldier who defeated the King of Norway; yet he is forced to try to come to terms with the fallen being who was murdered while lying on the earth and now resides beneath it like an 'old mole'. His father's **paradoxical** positioning as both high and low makes him a representative of the human race generally – 'a man…all in all'. His role, apart from being the obvious catalyst for the action and Hamlet's need to adopt 'an antic disposition', is to represent the theme of memory in several ways: Gertrude's failure to remember her first husband; Hamlet's exaggerated memory of his father as 'Hyperion' and distortion of time when assessing how long he has been dead; Hamlet's difficulty in remembering the injunction of the Ghost, who demands to be remembered at the first meeting and reappears to chastise Hamlet for having forgotten him; the fickleness of time-servers, who quickly forget their old master when a new one comes along. As a victim of fratricide, he is the first and worst kind of murder victim, evidence that any bond can be broken if the prize is valuable enough. On a simpler level, the Ghost is crucial to the gothic atmosphere of the play and its gripping beginning.

Act I scene 5

The Ghost tells Hamlet the story of how he was murdered while asleep and without benefit of last rites, and demands that Hamlet avenge his death. Hamlet extracts a vow of secrecy from his friends and warns them that he may feign madness henceforth.

Old Hamlet is the traditional chivalric warrior in his suit of armour, desire for revenge, and wish to spare Gertrude any blame. (Because women lacked reason they could not be considered fully responsible for their actions, and if not culpable then they were not

punishable.) By contrast we see Claudius as one of a new breed of **Machiavellian** non-combatant political statesmen. The Ghost shares with Hamlet the diction of 'prison', 'ears', 'weed', 'custom', 'seeming'. Poisoning through the ear – apart from providing a useful metaphorical parallel – may be a reference to the murder in 1538 of the Duke of Urbino, allegedly by this method. His final injunction, 'Remember me!', is a poignant and central one, provoking Hamlet's second **soliloquy** on the subject and the oath to wipe away his past and 'all trivial fond records' (l. 99), which include Ophelia. The world has shifted and Hamlet's friends find a different and disturbed man of 'wild and whirling words' (l. 133) when they catch up with him. He now knows what he previously suspected, which is that his uncle is a villain and that there is knowledge beyond mortal reach, even that of a philosopher. As Coleridge points out, 'Terror is closely connected with the ludicrous; the latter is the common mode by which the mind tries to emancipate itself from terror, so that Hamlet's wildness is but *half-false*' (in Hawkes, p. 176). His first instinct is to believe that it is 'an honest ghost' and that he has been chosen by fate to put right the wrongs in Denmark, which is enough to make anyone feel 'distracted'. And as Laurence Lerner points out, his problem is not only that he is 'a man who has to avenge his father, but 'a man who has been given a task by a ghost' (p. 70).

Act II scene 1

Polonius sends Reynaldo to gather information on his son's behaviour in Paris. Ophelia reports a disturbing encounter with Hamlet in her room.

Some time has passed, long enough for Hamlet's behaviour to have deteriorated to the point that Claudius has sent for Rosencrantz and Guildenstern, and for Laertes to have returned to Paris and be in need of money. The spying motif is shockingly evident here in Polonius's distrust of his own son. 'Encompassments' and subterfuge are symptomatic of the Danish court under Claudius, whose chief adviser and supporter loses the thread of his argument through being so periphrastic and prolix in his attempt to 'By indirections find directions out' (l. 66). Coleridge describes Polonius in this scene as 'the skeleton of his own former skill and statecraft' (Hawkes, p. 166). It is revealing that drinking and drabbing (frequenting brothels) are not considered immoral behaviour by Polonius, but we know that Hamlet has a lower tolerance of these male vices. Fencing, however, was viewed as a debased form of the originally noble art of jousting and was associated with wild, idle and loose living, especially gambling and quarrelling, hence Polonius's suspicion of Laertes.

Hamlet's growing distrust of words is strongly conveyed by his silent appraisal of Ophelia. His behaviour is that of a ghost 'loosèd out of hell' (l. 83); he is playing not only his own double in being a ghost of his former self, but also that of his father's ghost, appearing unsummoned and oddly attired. (The clothing of the mad was stereotypically disordered.) His rejection of Ophelia has been prepared for by his announcement in the previous scene that he will erase all trivial memories. It would not seem appropriate or respectful, given what he now knows, to continue a love affair and he has now lost his ability to trust even those nearest his heart. Perhaps he believes that she has failed the test of love and loyalty by returning his letters, or perhaps this is simply his fond farewell to her and his hopes of marriage, though his later treatment of her shows disappointment and anger towards her and her sex, and he may therefore already realise that she is doing her father's bidding.

Act II scene 2

Claudius conscripts Rosencrantz and Guildenstern, who were schoolfellows brought up with him, to probe Hamlet's condition. Ambassadors return from Norway to report success in having deflected the impending attack by young Fortinbras. Polonius plans with Claudius to eavesdrop on Hamlet and Ophelia to prove his theory that Hamlet is mad from unrequited love. After hearing of the arrival of the Players and requesting the recitation of a revenge speech, Hamlet arranges for the troupe to perform a murder play to test the Ghost's honesty through Claudius's reaction to it. Hamlet reproaches himself when alone for his delay.

The action of Acts II and III is continuous (*The Murder of Gonzago* is performed the day after the arrival of the Players). It has to be assumed that more than two months have passed since the opening of the play, since there is a reference in Act III scene 2 to Hamlet's father's death being 'twice two months' ago whereas at the beginning of Act I scene 2 it was allegedly less than two months. There is a reference to Lent in line 316, which may be metaphorical but would actually fit the time lapse from Christmas to the end of February or early March, which is when Lent falls. Rosencrantz's and Guildenstern's journey to Denmark, on horseback, after they were sent for by a messenger when Claudius realised there was a problem with Hamlet's attitude, could not have taken less than this amount of time; and during this time Hamlet's appearance and behaviour have apparently markedly altered. This indistinguishable pair of spies is a physical manifestation of duality in the play and the best evidence of Claudius's cynical, manipulative use of relationships. They are pawns in the power struggle between Claudius and Hamlet, without any existence beyond their obedience and fawning, like a pair of performing dogs. Hamlet's contempt for them is absolute, and their deaths are 'not near [his] conscience'. However, they are not in control of their fates, and can be seen as victims of a social system in which a royal summons cannot be refused.

Hamlet's love letter to Ophelia is the first objective, if retrospective, information about their relationship. The key word in the one which Polonius reads out is 'Doubt', but the sentiment seems sincere, despite the literary criticism of Polonius, who sees Hamlet as a lover who has fallen from sadness to madness in a traditional way. It is tempting fate – or conniving in his own destruction as Hamlet sees it – for the hubristic Polonius to invite the gods to 'Take this from this' (his head from his shoulders, l. 156) if he should prove to be wrong. Hamlet's insult of 'fishmonger' (l. 174) has given some editors a headache (and is inadequately glossed in the Penguin edition). It could refer to Hamlet's awareness that Polonius is 'fishing' for his secret; to men's belief that female private parts smell fishy; to the folk wisdom that fishmongers' daughters were easy conceivers and prolific breeders; or it could be a **pun** on 'fleshmonger' and therefore an imputation that Polonius is a bawd prostituting his daughter. All of these are relevant interpretations. Hamlet's preoccupation here is with mating and fleshly corruption, which bring evil into the world through child-bearing. Jephthah (l. 402) is a biblical paternal figure, a Judge of Israel, who sacrificed his daughter after depriving her of a husband, allowing her three months to bewail her virginity first. In addressing Polonius (for whom he has nothing but contempt) mockingly with this name, Hamlet is showing an awareness that Ophelia is in fact the victim of her father's manipulation. Jephthah's daughter was at the time the subject of a popular ballad. The reference prefigures Ophelia's maidenly death and makes it the more ironic that Hamlet should suspect her of the sexual promiscuity transferred from his mother. As well as containing bawdy references to female anatomy, this exchange continues the related **imagery** of graves, earth and prisons.

Shakespeare's company was feeling the competition of child actors at the Blackfriars theatre at this time. We can infer, however, that they are also a **metaphor** for usurpation, and that it is his uncle's stealing of the stage from himself and overacting that he is also thinking of. The Dido play, which may have served Shakespeare as a model, was written by Christopher Marlowe and Thomas Nashe (1594), but comes ultimately from Virgil's *Aeneid* and was a well-known episode in the fall of Troy narrative. Pyrrhus is a Greek hero avenging the death of his father Achilles, who had been killed by Priam's son Paris (stealer of Helen, an unfaithful wife) to avenge the slaying of his brother Hector. Through this drama Hamlet relives the family tragedy of the ruthless young pretender killing the helpless and beloved patriarch. The difference is that King Priam's queen, Hecuba, is beside herself with grief when she is bereaved, which is how Hamlet believes his mother should have reacted towards his father's death; he is moved to tears by the contrast, which also affects the audience.

The grand epic style of this play is suitably distinct from the style of Shakespeare's play, and the fact that Pyrrhus and Lucianus are fictional characters makes Hamlet and his situation seem nearer to reality in the audience's perception and his own. He enjoys the majesty and poetry of the archaic epic language – unlike the philistine Polonius – which is justified by the events of the tragedy: the fall of heroes in battle and the end of a dynasty and an era.

Hamlet takes over with relish and relief the role of director, a temporary escape from his predicament that gives him some control and power over events, a means of probing and trialling everyone else, and a chance to turn the tables on Claudius. The relationships between words and feelings and words and actions, and the difference between the genuine and the affected, are woven in complex and ironic ways within this scene, as Hamlet points out in his soliloquy.

Act III scene 1

Rosencrantz and Guildenstern report on Hamlet. Claudius and Polonius spy on the staged meeting between Hamlet and Ophelia, during which Hamlet abuses her for being a deceiver of men. Claudius realises that Polonius's diagnosis of Hamlet's malady is incorrect and determines to send him abroad. Polonius does not accept that he is mistaken and plans another spying session on a closet meeting between Hamlet and Gertrude.

This scene – called the nunnery scene – contains the first indication that Claudius is indeed guilty of the crime attributed to him and that his conscience is not extinct (ll. 50–54), though this **aside** is often cut in performance or not treated as an aside. It is also the first meeting between Hamlet and Ophelia that the audience is privy to. A nunnery was a term for a brothel in Elizabethan parlance, and this secondary meaning would be consistent with Hamlet's harsh wit and the use of double meanings in the play. The word also functions as a reminder of the limited choices available to respectable women: wife, widow or nun. If they are not to be allowed to make fools of men with marriage, and become breeders of sinners, then only the third option remains; Hamlet tells Ophelia eight times in Q1 to go to a nunnery. That she is being made a scapegoat for women's collective sins is shown in the shift from 'thee' to 'your' and from **verse** to prose in line 143. But his attack is not only against her or women generally, since he also expresses his contempt for men, including himself, who are all 'arrant knaves' (l. 129) 'crawling between earth and heaven' (l. 128). In attempting to return his 'remembrances' Ophelia is doing to him what he has done to her, wiping away their previous relationship, but he believes he has cause whereas she is simply obeying her odious father. Coleridge points out (see Hawkes, p. 169) that Hamlet's continuing spite towards Polonius could be evidence of his love for Ophelia as well as of his (correct) belief that Polonius supported Claudius in his marriage (i.e. Hamlet has a double reason to hate Polonius, for depriving him of both his mother and his lover).

There is much dispute between directors as to how the nunnery scene in Act III scene 1 should be played, depending on what they think Hamlet's feelings for Ophelia are at this point, and how much he is aware of:

1 Is he deliberately trying to distance her, being cruel only to be kind, because he cares enough about her to wish to spare her future pain and knows that there is no future in their relationship?

2 Is he trying to punish her for returning his letters and because he is now disgusted by all women?

3 Does he want her to break free from her father and go to a nunnery for her own salvation?

4 Is he simply trying to convince her that he is mad because he doesn't trust her?

5 Is he playing to the audience of her father and his stepfather, his remarks really meant for them not her (just as his bawdy comments to her in the Mousetrap scene are really meant for his mother)?

6 Does he wish to make Polonius look a fool in front of Claudius for believing he loves Ophelia?

Bear in mind that the Arden editors do not believe that Hamlet knows Claudius and Polonius are there, that there may be other possible reasons for his harsh words to Ophelia, and that he may not even be consistent in his feelings or body language during their encounter.

Whatever the intention of this contested scene – and it is likely to be a complex and contradictory mixture of conscious and unconscious attitudes and feelings – Hamlet does convince Ophelia that he is mad (hence her lamentation for his 'o'erthrown' (l. 151) mind). The Arden editors believe it is unclear whether or not Hamlet is aware that Ophelia is being used to make him reveal his secrets, because of the **ambiguity** of his question 'Where's your father?' (l. 130), which may be triggered either by his remembering him because of his attack on liars or by the sudden realisation of where Polonius is. Furthermore, Hamlet entangles father and daughter and treats them as a double creature in his utterances to both of them, so it is not surprising that he should think of Polonius here. It was an Elizabethan dramatic convention that those spied upon were never aware of it, and there are many other instances in Shakespeare where this is so. However, if Hamlet is not aware of being spied upon, then our estimation of his intelligence is reduced, and it would seem to be inconsistent with his 'prophetic soul' and awareness of other hidden agendas, such as the letter for England he somehow knows about in Act III scene 4. Coleridge points out (Hawkes, p. 185) that he begins his address to her with tenderness, but then, presumably realising that she is putting on an act for an audience of his enemies, breaks out into anger, condemnation and coarseness. Claudius, in contrast to his obtuse, opinionated and stubborn adviser, concludes that there is something more serious than a lover's tiff over which Hamlet's 'melancholy sits on brood' (l. 166).

Act III scene 2

Hamlet asks Horatio to observe Claudius during the play. He is insulting to Ophelia, Gertrude and Claudius before and during the performance. After the King has interrupted the play by walking out, thereby confirming his guilt, Hamlet is summoned by Rosencrantz and Guildenstern to the Queen's closet.

Hamlet praises Horatio's **Stoic** practice of treating all of 'Fortune's buffets and rewards' (l. 77) with equilibrium and refusing to be 'passion's slave', which reflects on his own character and belief of what a man should be. This central scene highlights the crime at the centre of the play, though it occurred before it began. St Augustine alluded to the cross of Christ as the mousetrap of the devil, who is trapped by his own corruption. No play called *The Murder of Gonzago* is known to have existed; it may have been inspired by the story of the death in October 1538 of the Duke of Urbino, who was poisoned by having a lotion put into his ears by his barber at the instigation of a kinsman of the Duchess. The form of the play, in **rhyming couplets**, employs medieval **rhetorical** devices such as **circumlocutio** and has a style characteristic of an older period, containing **sententiae**, syntactical inversions and archaic diction.

Hamlet's treatment of Ophelia, much harsher than any exchange hitherto, could be accounted for by his burden of all the things he wants to accuse his mother of, as she is within earshot and he has had no opportunity so far.

The dumb-show prologue, often cut, with its apparent redundancy, is a puzzle to critics. It is a silent parallel to the double of the play within a play and a mirror image of what happened to Hamlet's father, according to the Ghost's account. Since the play is interrupted, as Hamlet expects it will be, this is the only full version of the murder of Gonzago and is necessary for the understanding of both audiences. Lucianus doubles in Hamlet's mind as both Claudius in the past and himself in the hypothetical future – like Laertes and Fortinbras to follow and Pyrrhus already mentioned – as an avenger/killer figure. The dialogue is equally necessary, however, to convey the insincerity of the Player Queen. Commentators also wonder why Claudius does not react at this stage; they offer a choice of answers, from his (1) not having actually paid any attention to it, perhaps being distracted by concerns about Hamlet's excitable behaviour, to his (2) having seen it but not immediately recognised its import, to the (3) most commonly accepted 'second tooth' theory, i.e. that he could stand it once but not twice. He may well be in shock and unable to decide immediately how best to react, not knowing what we know. Since the prologues were rather stylised, perhaps the second theory is the more likely, supported by the fact that Ophelia has to ask Hamlet to explain it to her.

Hamlet is euphoric at the success of his 'false fire' (l. 275), as if he has already done the deed demanded of him with words alone. Certainly he is relieved to have his father's ghost proved honest and a doubt settled. He turns upon Rosencrantz and Guildenstern, Polonius and his mother with vehement sarcasm – ridiculously repeating the title 'mother' – and his brief fifth soliloquy gives the impression of renewed resolve. Until now he has been an onlooker of the play's action, but he now becomes an active protagonist, inspired by the First Player.

Act III scene 3

Claudius expedites in the interests of his own safety the plan to remove Hamlet to England. When alone, he tries to pray but cannot because he does not feel repentant. Hamlet sees him apparently praying and decides not to take this opportunity to kill him in case he would be sending his soul to heaven.

Claudius reveals in his soliloquy that he is fully aware that fratricide is the primal sin. He argues in a similar dialectical and rhetorical way to Hamlet, with doubles and contradictions, showing how ironically similar they are intellectually. The difference is that he cannot resist temptation or show remorse because his nature is more sensual and less capable of renunciation. Hamlet does not know what the audience knows when he delivers his sixth soliloquy, explaining why he must not kill Claudius while praying. Since we now realise that Claudius does at least wish he could pray, there may be a brief evocation of sympathy for him at this point, and even antipathy towards Hamlet, especially if we feel along with Dr Johnson that Hamlet's motive for prolonging the king's 'sickly days' is a shocking one, 'too horrible to be read or to be uttered'. However, given the way in which his father was taken 'full of bread', and the indisputable logic of it not being appropriate revenge to send the villain to heaven,

Hamlet's reasoning seems acceptable, though not remotely Christian. (He also makes sure later that Rosencrantz and Guildenstern are not allowed any 'shriving time'). But nor would it have been Christian to kill a man at prayer, with his back turned, unarmed, and possibly in a chapel – which has always symbolised sanctuary, whatever the crime.

Hamlet's putting up of his sword both echoes and contrasts with Pyrrhus holding his sword above Priam's head in Act II scene 2. However, the fact that he does attempt to kill the King a few moments later disproves critics such as Coleridge and Bradley who (citing the hypothetical tense of 'Now might I do it') assume this deferral is just another excuse on Hamlet's part for his failure to act or that he hasn't yet taken the decision to keep his promise to the Ghost. It is doubly ironic that it would have been a perfect opportunity, since Claudius is not in fact 'fit and seasoned for his passage', whereas his attempt to kill the King shortly afterwards is misdirected. A king was always guarded and it is difficult to see what opportunity Hamlet could have had so far to gain access to the suspicious King for the purpose of murdering him, a fact which detractors of Hamlet tend to overlook.

Act III scene 4

Gertrude, fearing for her safety, calls for help. The hidden Polonius gives himself away and Hamlet stabs him, assuming that it is the King who is eavesdropping in his mother's closet. The Ghost appears, unseen by Gertrude, to remind Hamlet of his task of revenge. Hamlet succeeds in awakening Gertrude's conscience and in convincing her that he is only 'mad in craft'.

Directors set this scene, known as the closet scene, in Gertrude's bedroom, presumably to stress the **Oedipal** nature of their relationship, but a closet was not a bedroom in Shakespeare's day and there would have been no bed on stage. However, it seems shocking that there should be a hidden audience for the only intimate exchange between mother and son in the play. **Stichomythia** is a classical device used for verbal sparring between adversaries. Gertrude cannot sustain the duel of words for very long, being inferior in word-play and understanding to Hamlet. It is appropriate that Polonius should cause his own death by being incapable of keeping quiet, as well as by his 'intruding' (l. 32). (A rat was thought to attract its own death by squeaking and drawing attention to itself.) There is a plausible critical view that Hamlet kills Polonius in a moment of genuine madness, at least in the sense of it being an uncharacteristically uncontrolled impulse. This is consistent with his later apology to Laertes at the end that the other Hamlet did it, though this may just be diplomacy, and with his weeping over his action afterwards, though we cannot know whether this is just Gertrude covering for him.

Directors must decide whether or not she suspected foul play to determine the exact tone in which she exclaims 'As kill a king!' (l. 31). The emphasis, however, is more on her sins of bad taste and sexual activity than on that of marrying a murderer. Some editors believe that this scene makes it clear that Gertrude was adulterous, but 'leave to feed' (l. 67) is ambiguous and does not necessarily imply that it was while old Hamlet was alive.

Hamlet, the sensitive only son, may well be feeling rejected by his mother (irrespective of Oedipus), a loss perhaps more keenly felt than that of the throne, and even of his father. Since Hamlet identifies himself so completely with his father, the replacement of his father in his mother's affections is tantamount to a rejection of Hamlet himself. This would explain his despondency, even before the additional knowledge that the perpetrator of his and his father's ousting was his uncle, whose taint comes too near to Hamlet, a close blood relation. It is precisely because his mother finds the brothers interchangeable that Hamlet is forced to see them as polar opposites and to describe his father in extreme terms of approbation.

According to Q1 the Ghost appears 'in his night gowne', i.e. no longer the armed general but the domestic husband. This befits his protectiveness towards Gertrude, but it seems harsh of him to berate Hamlet for forgetting his 'purpose' when he has just killed Polonius, believing him to be Claudius. Hamlet has disobeyed the Ghost by tackling his mother, and is punished by this second appearance. Critics have asked why Gertrude cannot see the Ghost. Muir (1963) suggests unconvincingly that it is because she has betrayed him (p. 43). It is, however, simply more dramatically effective for Hamlet to appear to be talking to thin air and involved in a two-way conversation, in touch with both the living and the dead and forming the blood link between them. In any case it is consistent with the Ghost's desire to spare his former wife that he would not wish to frighten her further. Hamlet sarcastically presents Gertrude with a list of double negatives (ll. 182–97) to convey his quasi-voyeuristic disgust at her physical intimacies with Claudius (see Waldock, Lerner p. 80). It is understandable here that Ernest Jones felt that Hamlet is obsessed with the images of his mother's relationship with his uncle (in Jump, p. 58).

This is a turning point in the play, in that Hamlet for the first time acts impulsively and trusts that the outcome was heaven-directed, saying that Polonius deserved his 'fortune' (l. 33). Hamlet is now causing rather than responding to events since his rash action forces Claudius to advance the plan to remove Hamlet from court to the following morning, and he is now committed to killing Claudius as he has revealed too much of his own knowledge and intentions by killing Polonius. He also saves his mother's soul by his power of speech and argument. The bond between mother and son has been restored by his confiding to her his feigned madness and by her willingness to obey him. The word 'mother', last word in the scene, is spoken in a very different tone from when he entered her closet. Hamlet seems to have accepted that 'knavery' (l. 206) is a necessary part of his role and of providence's plan for setting things right, and he no longer needs to moralise over or take responsibility for what happens.

Act IV scene 1

Gertrude tells Claudius that Hamlet has killed Polonius and blames his action on his madness. Rosencrantz and Guildenstern are instructed to find the body.

This scene is part of the continuous action and editors lament the traditional break between acts here, often used as the interval. Gertrude has now also become an actor, as she must

hide from Claudius what she now knows. Act IV is a fast-moving sequence of events and battalions of sorrows succeeding each other, which is typical of the tragedies but particularly striking in one which is previously predicated upon delay and inaction. The conspicuous use of the royal plural in this scene suggests that Claudius now feels insecure and targeted by Hamlet's 'poisoned shot' (l. 43).

Act IV scene 2

Hamlet refuses to tell Rosencrantz and Guildenstern where Polonius is 'stowed' and he berates them for being the disposable minions of Claudius.

Rosencrantz and Guildenstern lose any claim to audience sympathy here, especially when we compare their apparently willing collaboration with the role of Horatio in the court. Hamlet's talk of bodies refers to the fact that a king, as head of state and church, was ascribed two bodies, a corporeal one and a corporate one representing the body politic. Hamlet may here be threatening, while feigning madness, that although Claudius may appear to have taken on the role of king, it is an illegitimate usurpation which does not bring the two bodies into alignment; and that he is about to forfeit both of them (one already prefigured by the dead body of Polonius, which has become separated and distant from the dignity of the office he held).

Act IV scene 3

Rosencrantz and Guildenstern report back to Claudius their failure to discover the whereabouts of the body. Hamlet tells Claudius himself, and is informed that he is to be sent to England for his own safety. When alone, Claudius reveals that he has ordered the death of Hamlet on his arrival in England.

The contempt for Polonius's corpse, and description of it being eaten, is a leftover from the Saxo **source**. However, it is consistent with Hamlet's interest in the absolute difference between being alive and being dead, and death's erosion of the distinction between kings and beggars, who are but two different dishes in the same meal. Hamlet does not dignify his stepfather with verse. There is no evidence that Rosencrantz and Guildenstern have seen through Claudius or realise that Hamlet is being sent to his death.

Act IV scene 4

Hamlet meets the captain of the Norwegian army, led by Fortinbras, and learns that the army is en route for Poland in order to fight for a small piece of disputed land.

This scene was omitted from performances from 1676 until the end of the nineteenth century, thereby removing Hamlet's last soliloquy. Disease and food and earth imagery abound in this scene (linked previously by worms). The seventh and final soliloquy conveys Hamlet's conclusion that honour is what distinguishes men from beasts and heroes from ordinary mortals. Debate and conscience are inconsequential in both senses, and only action fulfils ambition and wins a permanent place in memory and history. From now on Hamlet is a soldier who unquestioningly obeys commands from a higher authority. Hamlet possibly admires Fortinbras for being absolute in 'find[ing] quarrel in a straw/When honour's at the stake' (ll. 55–6), but he is arguably no better than a 'barbarous adventurer' (Muir 1972, p. 63). He represents the traditional honour code of being willing to risk everything for glory and a plot of land, and is not burdened by intellectual or moral considerations. Hamlet and the audience make comparisons between the two fatherless princes with usurping uncles; although they pay tribute to each other, they have very different approaches to life which are difficult to reconcile. Fortinbras is the opportunist and avenging warrior; Hamlet is the philosopher with a conscience and a dread of committing an act of injustice, even when he knows with his 'prophetic soul' that he is the victim of one. Like Laertes, the physically daring Fortinbras represents humanity on a more primitive and simple level of existence, responding to violence with violence.

Act IV scene 5

Ophelia is reported to have gone mad and appears on stage to sing songs of love and loss. Laertes, with a band of rebels, bursts in to demand vengeance for the death of his father. Claudius skilfully calms him down but when Ophelia reappears to give out herbs to the assembled company his grief and fury are reignited.

It may now be early summer, given the flowers available to Ophelia and the time required for Hamlet to have returned from his aborted voyage to England. It seems odd and unnecessary for Horatio to be in this scene, and it may have been the expediency of doubling up actors which caused him to be used in Q2 but not Q1. The loss of her father and her lover have become synthesised as a double grief for Ophelia, and she has become her own double, 'Divided from herself' in being in her madness both sexually explicit and still an innocent maiden, who represents herself with flowers in the pastoral tradition. Flowers, like skulls, were a **memento mori** and evoke **pathos**. The songs, like the herbs, seem specifically directed: a dead unmourned lover for Gertrude; a seduction song for Claudius; a funeral **elegy** for the son of the dead man. The herbs are nature's cure for ailments and relevant to their recipients: remembrance (rosemary), thoughts (pansies), flattery (fennel), sorrow (columbines), regret (rue), deception (daisies), faithfulness (violets). She previews her own death in her last song, welcoming her 'deathbed' because 'he is dead'.

Custom is overturned by Laertes and his revolutionary rabble, and the usurper Claudius is fittingly threatened with usurpation. In contrast to Hamlet, Laertes unthinkingly dares damnation and gives way to public passion, bombastic expression and stereotypical lament. Laertes serves Claudius's will, not that of heaven, and his gullibility and thoughtlessness make the audience respect Hamlet's perception and caution the more by comparison. For Laertes, honour is a matter of outward show, trappings and suits. He is at least as bothered by the lack of ceremony at the funeral of his father as about the manner of his death, which shows again in relation to Ophelia's burial. Gertrude's insult to Laertes

that he is a 'false Danish dog' (l. 112) has given rise to speculation that like many European royal consorts at this time – including the Danish wife of James I – Gertrude is a foreigner, i.e. not Danish. This would add further complexity to her position and make Hamlet's blood 'commeddled' (III.2.79). Like Polonius, Claudius ironically and hubristically calls down his own punishment by inviting the 'great axe' to fall (l. 218).

Act IV scene 6

Sailors give Horatio a letter from Hamlet telling of his capture by pirates and imminent return.

The letter reports a battle at sea and the unexpected doubling back of Hamlet, an arrow returned to plague the inventor, a current turned awry, which proves heaven is 'ordinant'.

Act IV scene 7

Claudius receives a letter from Hamlet notifying him of his impending return. Claudius persuades Laertes not only to believe that Hamlet is his enemy but to fight a dishonourable duel with him using an 'unbated' and poisoned rapier. Gertrude announces and describes the death by drowning of Ophelia.

Claudius the politician has an answer to all of Laertes's charges, and gives two reasons why he could not punish Hamlet directly for the murder of Polonius. Neither should be believed, since the claim that Hamlet was 'envenomed' by envy against Laertes after the report of Lamord is unlikely to be true on several counts. The Frenchman's name means 'death', which is coming to the three men who know of him. Hamlet is in double danger by having a joint adversary in Claudius and Laertes, who both wish him dead, and their plot involves both rapier and poison, the latter doubly administered on a foil tip and in a wine goblet. Claudius easily manipulates the credulous Laertes into taking on the task of disposing of Hamlet by making his willingness to murder him a test of his love for his father. This is a temptation scene in which Laertes is seduced through his own vaingloriousness. Claudius does not mention that he has already arranged for Hamlet's death, but was perhaps going to do so at line 35, before yet another interruption. The reading of line 56 as 'Thus didest thou' was disputed by the previous editor of the Arden edition, who believes that the play has been impoverished for over three and a half centuries by this misreading for 'Thus diest thou' (supported by the Q1 text).

Gertrude's narrative **elegy** to Ophelia beautifies and dramatises her death; she speaks as though she witnessed it, and someone must have done – in keeping with all the other scenes in the play which have spectators. Ophelia's descent from air (tree branch) to water ('weeping brook') to earth ('muddy death'), caused by her heaviness (waterlogged garments), is a paradigm of the play's use of the elemental and chain-of-being hierarchies and of Hamlet's view of the downward course of mankind. The willow was traditionally the tree from which girls who had lost their lovers made mourning garlands; it adds to the pathos of her end that she was unknowingly making her own burial wreath while singing her own funeral hymn.

Act V scene 1

Two locals question whether Ophelia should have been granted a Christian burial. Hamlet is discussing mortality with the gravedigger when the funeral procession for Ophelia arrives in the churchyard. Hamlet and Laertes fight until they are parted.

This is probably the day after Ophelia's death, because Hamlet has not yet met Claudius since his return, neither he nor Horatio has learnt of Ophelia's death, and bodies were buried quickly at that time, for obvious sanitary reasons. It is only a tradition – but a long one – that both Clowns are gravediggers, although line 14 suggests not, and one leaves as Hamlet arrives. The memorable role of the riddling sexton was created for Robert Armin, Kemp's comic successor. 'Clown' in Elizabethan could simply mean 'rustic', but the additional sense of comedian is useful for **irony** and doubleness in a tragic scene. In some editions they are called the first and second gravediggers, since this is their function and relevance to the play: they dig holes in the earth to lower men into. They are instrumental in reminding the audience of Adam, the first digger ('Delver') and fallen man, and in re-inforcing the play's language (**puns**, quibbles, questions) and themes (doubt, **ambiguity**, equivocation). This pair of entertainers, cod philosophers and barrack-room lawyers perform on their earthy stage for the unseen audience of Hamlet and Horatio until line 115. Their questioning of the legal and Christian acceptability or otherwise of Ophelia's cause of death makes the audience aware of the doubt concerning it and the difficulty of estab-lishing the truth about anything, and furthers the debate of salvation versus damnation. The songs echo those of the future incumbent of the grave in the previous scene: how quickly love and life become loss and death. Hamlet's conversation with the Clown is interrupted by the funeral procession, as death interrupts life.

The body of a suicide or murderer could not be buried within hallowed ground, hence the priest's reluctance to give Ophelia a proper burial. The bizarre legal **paradox** is that she is only entitled to a Christian burial if she drowned herself in self-defence. This is a parody of a philosophical debate, but the verbs 'to act, to do, and to perform' (l. 12) are central to the play. The sentiment of the scene is firmly on the side of Ophelia having gone to her grave a virgin, evoking a sense of tragic loss and waste, and reduces the credibility of the critical argument for her having been seduced, made pregnant, abandoned, and forced to commit suicide.

We have escaped the constrained atmosphere of the court and see Hamlet here as a man of the people, able to share their concerns and speak to them as an equal. He has the common touch, and more in common with the honesty and wit of the Clowns/grave-diggers than with the pomposity and affectation of corrupt courtiers. Hamlet is in a sense attending his own funeral (as in the Saxo source) in that he is identifying with Ophelia and Yorick, and by revealing his presence to Claudius and Laertes he is signing his own death

warrant. Claudius appears in his final words in the scene to be threatening to turn him into that paradoxical thing, a 'living monument' (l. 293) for Ophelia's grave. In the interim, however, he will pluck the mantle of the ruler from the usurper Claudius, and for however brief a moment he will be 'Hamlet the Dane' (l. 254), King of Denmark.

All scenes in the play have led the protagonist to this place, where he must face 'Goodman Delver', the figure of Adam who was the first man to bear arms with which to dig and to fight battles, the man of clay who must return to clay and by being 'shipped into the land'. The ghost rose from his grave here in this earth to summon his son to join him. But the convergence of the twain, twin lines of fate, can be traced further back, since old Fortinbras was killed by old Hamlet on the same day that young Hamlet began his life, so it is fitting that on the day of young Hamlet's death and committal to a plot of earth, young Fortinbras can avenge his dead father and his lost land by taking over the throne of Denmark.

Hamlet has his moment of **anagnorisis** here, recognising with regret the truly fallen state of man, whether he be Yorick the fool or Alexander the Great, and the power of nature and fate, stronger than any human, hero or god. Life is brief whatever happens, and what matters is to leave it honourably, even if, or perhaps especially if, 'betimes'. He foresees his fate in that of Yorick, the beloved former jester at the court of Elsinore whose role he has been playing. It answers Hamlet's question of 'What is a man' (IV.4.33) to see what he must inevitably become, and to realise that the only thing to distinguish one from another is his reputation, his honour that lives on beyond his interment in the memories of those who live on to tell the tale. Words and rank, quiddities and indentures, are transient and worthless in the face of the skull, the concrete **memento mori** image and undeniable physical proof of mortality and decomposition.

Laertes is his father's son in his use of hollow **rhetoric** and bombastic diction laced with classical references to enhance sentiment, and his melodramatic delivery (ll. 243–50) provokes Hamlet to parody his declamatory style, that of the old Revenge plays and one which Hamlet has already condemned in Act III scene 2 as worthless ranting. Hamlet warns Laertes that he has in him 'something dangerous' (l. 258), presumably his commitment to his fate which makes death a matter of indifference to him: 'it is no matter' (l. 286) is now his philosophy. This is the first time in the play that Hamlet and Laertes meet face to face, though their two lines have been on a convergence since the beginning because of their shared aims, feelings and experiences. Their duel to the death begins here, in a grave, each claiming the right to the patch of ground for having loved Ophelia more than the other.

This graveyard scene has no equal in Shakespeare for its range of pathos, wit, irony, comedy, psychology, legal debate, political topicality, metaphysical speculation – and possibly biographical references to Shakespeare's father, who was a tanner/glovemaker. In a play full of plays, this is another self-contained drama which not only has all of the above elements, but contains the full range of verse and prose styles, touches on all the themes of the work, and also provides a visual paradigm of all its imagery. The two doomed sons engage in battle, verbally and physically, in a 'pit of clay' and surrounded by skulls, as departed loved ones and the mythically and historically mighty hover as a reminder of the lowly and decomposed state to which we shall all inevitably be reduced.

Act V scene 2

Hamlet explains to Horatio how he switched letters on the ship and substituted an order for the execution of Rosencrantz and Guildenstern for his own. He mocks the affected courtier Osrick but accepts his stepfather's invitation to a duel with Laertes, in which the foils are exchanged by mistake and both parties fatally wounded. Gertrude drinks the poisoned wine intended for Hamlet and dies. Hamlet kills Laertes with the poisoned sword, then Claudius with the sword and the wine. As Hamlet dies, he names Fortinbras as successor to the throne and persuades Horatio to live to tell his tale rather than join him in death. The English ambassadors arrive to announce the death of Rosencrantz and Guildenstern; Fortinbras arrives with his army to claim Denmark and orders a hero's funeral for Hamlet.

Hamlet is now convinced that 'There's a divinity that shapes our ends' (l. 10), a design in the ordering of the universe which renders human intentions futile. By chance (but 'even in that was heaven ordinant' l. 48) he had his father's signet ring on him and, doubling for Claudius, was thus able to forge the substitute letter.

Osrick is the new Polonius, a sycophantic and shallow show-off with a place at court based merely on the ownership of land. His role here, with his farcical 'bonnet', is comic, as an ironic prologue to the tragedy to follow. It seems painfully unjust that the worthless Osrick, replacement for Polonius in stupidity, pomposity and prosiness, should live while Hamlet must die. Critics have been much exercised by the problematical maths of the wager, but it is not necessary to understand the exact terms, only that Claudius is ironically supporting Hamlet and betting on him to not allow Laertes to exceed him by more than three hits.

Hamlet's refusal to 'peruse the foils' (IV.7.135) cannot be attributed to his trusting nature in the circumstances, since he has had a premonition of something 'ill'; it must therefore be interpreted as an abdication of free will in the service of providence. There is no defying augury; what must happen will happen, sooner or later. His words 'The readiness is all' (l. 216) echo Matthew chapter 24 verse 44 and Luke chapter 12 verse 40. 'Let be' (l. 218 and in the Q2 text only) is taken to be a philosophical and Christian expression in keeping with Hamlet's new resigned mood. It could, however, be a breaking off and command for silence because of the arrival of the procession, which would be a typical interruption and make the phrase characteristically ambiguous.

When Hamlet apologises to Laertes it may not be as hypocritical as some critics (including Dr Johnson) have claimed, since although he was not genuinely mad he may genuinely regret the frenzy of ungovernable 'passion' that made him a murderer, and it is possible that he really did weep for what he did, knowing his mood changes. We know Hamlet has regard for Laertes as a 'noble youth' (V.1.220), and the word 'brother' is a

strong indication that Hamlet feels a bond with Laertes at this time – as a fellow mourner of Ophelia and picture of his own loss – and wishes to be reconciled to him before death; Laertes would have become Hamlet's brother if a marriage with Ophelia had taken place.

The duel scene is the manifestation of the **metaphorical** battle of good versus evil conducted on every level: Prince Hamlet is fighting for his father, for Denmark, and for Christianity; Laertes is surrogate for the evil king in the battle of 'mighty opposites' (l. 62). Hamlet's thinking has come full circle: he now fears damnation if he continues to allow 'this canker of our nature come/In further evil' (ll. 69–70), and so dispatches his duplicitous stepfather with a double dose of poison, doubly requiting his father.

It is odd that Hamlet does not mention the Ghost in the last two acts of the play, and he never actually accuses Claudius of the murder of his father, even when about to kill him; 'incestuous, murderous, damnèd Dane' (l. 319) would apply to Claudius's treatment of his mother alone. There are critics who believe that Hamlet has ceased to mention the Ghost because he has realised that his father belonged to the old school, one which pursued honour at whatever cost to human life, an ethic which is now distasteful to him. In that case his nomination of Fortinbras to fill the vacuum must be either bitterly ironic or prophetically pragmatic; who else is there to hand the country over to but the person from whom it was being defended at the beginning of the play, who has come to take it anyway, and who may turn out to be more ruthless than Claudius? This, however, sits uneasily with the traditional plot resolution expected of a **tragedy**, when the time for sardonic speeches is over and a hopeful note for the future is struck. But as Hamlet is aware, killing a king, however bad or illegitimate, is treason, for which there will be punitive consequences, and Fortinbras may well turn out to be more ruthless than Claudius. The story is left incomplete, and needs a Horatio to fill in the gaps for those who remain; those who are dead have departed in a state of 'bestial oblivion'. Horatio's **eulogy** for Hamlet appears to be curtailed by the entrance of Fortinbras.

Gertrude's refusal to obey Claudius over the drink, with which she wishes to toast Hamlet, suggests she now ranks her son higher than her new husband in her affections and duty, and wishes to show her loyalty to him and reject the King's authority. Some commentators think she is deliberately killing herself as a punishment or in order to join her former husband, but for it to be suicide she would need to know of the poison plot against Hamlet, and there is no evidence for this.

Hamlet speaks in this final scene as one who has learnt to embrace the Calvinist doctrine of predestination and 'recognizes the folly and pretension of humanistic aspiration, and acknowledges the controlling power of God' (introduction to Penguin edition, p. xxxvi). As C. S. Lewis points out, this is where the Hamlet who lost his way before the play began finds it again, and knows his true direction (Lerner, p. 72). 'Ripeness is all' is a philosophical conclusion which accepts the notion of a higher power, and one worthy of respect. What is important to Hamlet the intellectual is the ability to discern a pattern in the workings of the universe, for otherwise there is only chaos and nothing has any purpose or meaning.

Any pattern is better than no pattern, and by the end Hamlet has ceased to doubt or question, and seems at peace with himself. By seeming to succumb to God's will he has actually achieved his own. Alternatively, it could be argued that Hamlet's capitulation at the end to the whims of providence is a betrayal of all his former noble principles. Horatio advises him 'If your mind dislike anything, obey it' (l. 211), so this could be seen as a kind of suicide after all. Hamlet has even less reason to wish to live now, with Ophelia gone. The third interpretation is that Hamlet's error is in having delayed, and that had he dispatched Claudius earlier he might not have had to give his own life to do so now, and so he is paying the price of his procrastination.

It is fitting that Hamlet's final utterance should be incomplete, interrupted by his dying. Words are ultimately inadequate and imperfect: '– the rest is silence' (l. 352). He dies an honourable death as a man of action and on a battlefield, a Christian soldier who has proved himself obedient and no coward, who has done his appointed duty, and who has put time back in its joint. That Horatio, the stoic and Aristotelian, offers to kill himself is testimony to the exceptional qualities of Hamlet, the 'sweet Prince', and to the strength of their friendship. Unlike Laertes, Horatio is not 'passion's slave' and therefore his being overcome by emotion has the greater impact. However, his simplistic, conventional summary of the events shows that he hasn't really understood. Hamlet briefly becomes King of Denmark, entitled to a royal send-off and to nominate his successor. Fortinbras returns the compliment by ironically stating that Hamlet would have made a good king. He is granted a soldier's funeral, a recognition that he is his father's son, and worthy of elevation; the gun salute releases his soul to fly to heaven.

Characters

Prince Hamlet

Hamlet is the only child of Gertrude and the recently deceased King Hamlet of Denmark. At Elsinore, the royal court of Denmark, for his father's funeral and his mother's marriage to his father's brother, he is refused permission by his new stepfather to return to the University of Wittenberg in Germany to continue his studies. As an intellectual, he loves truth, desires honour, collides with doubt, and suffers from his continuous struggle with instincts and passions. After much heart-searching, reflection, and testing of humans, ghosts and the gods, Hamlet accepts that it is his destiny to rid Denmark of the corruption introduced by his uncle's crime of fratricide, which was revealed to him by his father's spirit. He dies in a duel with Laertes, whom he kills, but not before finally avenging his father's death by stabbing and poisoning his uncle Claudius. For a few minutes he inherits the throne of Denmark, before being replaced by Fortinbras of Norway. The name Hamnet/Hamlet was a significant one for Shakespeare as it belonged to his only son, who died in 1596 at the age of 11.

King Claudius

Claudius is the brother (presumed younger) of the former King of Denmark, whom he relieved of his throne and his wife by poison and a hasty remarriage following an apparently adulterous relationship. He belatedly reveals that he has some feelings of guilt for the murder, but not enough to make him confess, repent or renounce his ill-gotten gains. He is engaged from the beginning of the play in a duel of cunning with Hamlet, whose position as natural successor he has usurped. His political skills are considerable, and show clearly in his exploitation and manipulation of Polonius, Laertes, and Rosencrantz and Guildenstern. His scheming finally backfires when he is killed by the same poisoned sword that was used by Laertes to kill Hamlet, and by the poisoned wine that he prepared for Hamlet and that killed his wife.

Queen Gertrude

As wife, mistress, widow, sister-in-law, mother, and would-be mother-in-law, Gertrude has relationships with the key men and the only other female in the play, and it is the mixing of them that causes the central problem. She was allegedly unfaithful to Hamlet's father before his death, and seems to Hamlet to be insufficiently grief-stricken for him after it. She does not apparently realise, until Hamlet tells her in Act III, that her first husband was murdered by her second, after which she becomes remorseful and reconciled with her son, though still playing the public role of wife to Claudius. She dies after drinking from the poisoned chalice intended for Hamlet when toasting her son during the duel. A historicist reading equates her with the ageing Queen Elizabeth I.

The Ghost

The ghost of old Hamlet appears three times on stage and has reportedly appeared to the soldiers on watch at midnight the two previous nights prior to the start of the play. His appearance in full armour is a reminder of the war footing Denmark is now on, which is a result of his having defeated the old King of Norway in a duel and won lands, which the King of Norway's son intends to reclaim. The Ghost spends his days in purgatory, being punished for his sins, since his sudden death while sleeping meant that he died without absolution and was therefore unfit for heaven. Though he can be seen by Hamlet's companions of the watch, the Ghost chooses to be invisible to his widow when he makes his second and last appearance to Hamlet in her closet. He is a chivalrous ghost, and does not wish to distress Gertrude or for Hamlet to do so either, despite her faults. Though he precipitates the action of the play, he is not referred to again after Act III. Tradition has it that Shakespeare himself played this role originally. Shakespeare's own father died in September 1601.

Polonius

As counsellor to the King and father to Laertes and Ophelia, Polonius gives all of them plenty of pompous advice. He becomes convinced that Hamlet's madness is caused by unrequited love for Ophelia, after he has insisted that she return Hamlet's love letters to her on the grounds that Hamlet cannot have honourable intentions. He is thanked by Claudius in the first court scene for having facilitated the hasty marriage, and is a sycophantic and tireless supporter of the new king until Hamlet stabs him by mistake while he is eavesdropping in Gertrude's closet. His critical, interfering, **philistine** and self-righteous nature is reminiscent of the Puritans, who were against the theatre, which would explain Shakespeare's and Hamlet's satirical animosity towards him. It has been suggested that he is a caricature of Lord Burghley, Queen Elizabeth's Lord Treasurer, chief courtier and spymaster (who is known to have spied on his son Thomas Cecil in Paris). He is traditionally played as a comic character, but more recent productions have emphasised his sinister side.

Laertes

He has been in Paris and is given leave by Claudius to return there. He returns to Elsinore to avenge his father's death when he receives news of it. He is thereafter a witness to the madness of his sister Ophelia and attends her funeral, which he considers inadequate. Claudius persuades him that Hamlet is his enemy and they plot together to get rid of him by means of a fencing match when they learn of Hamlet's unexpected return from his voyage to England. When both Hamlet and himself have received their death wounds from the envenomed rapier, Laertes tells Hamlet that 'the King's to blame', provoking him to turn the weapon on Claudius.

Ophelia

She is subject to her father's wishes and demand for obedience. She is friendless, motherless and without support once her brother Laertes returns to Paris, Hamlet rejects her, and her father is killed. She descends into madness following her father's funeral and Hamlet's removal from court. She drowns when she falls from a tree over a stream. Her burial service is conducted with 'maimed rites' because the church suspects suicide, though the coroner pronounced that her death was accidental. Hamlet declares in public at her graveside that he did truly love her.

Horatio

Apparently a Dane, Horatio is a fellow student of Hamlet's at Wittenberg and an old friend of his. He came to Elsinore for old Hamlet's funeral, and is still there several weeks later, when he gives Hamlet the message that his father's ghost has appeared on the battlements. He is present during part of the encounter between Hamlet and the Ghost. He starts out not believing in ghosts but is shown that there are 'more things in heaven and earth' than philosophy can explain. He is an unimaginative, dispassionate and staunch ally of the distracted prince. His loyalty in an otherwise corrupted court redeems humanity and the bond of friendship.

Despite his stoicism he is moved to offer to die with Hamlet, but is instead tasked with telling the tale of Hamlet's death and observing his memory, as the only significant Danish survivor. He has little use for words, which are the tool of sycophants, politicians and seducers, speaking rarely and only when spoken to or provoked by events.

Rosencrantz and Guildenstern

This inseparable duo has well-known Danish names with Christian **symbolism**: crown of roses, i.e. thorns (and also a reference to the Catholic rosary) and golden star respectively. They are childhood friends and 'old schoolfellows' of Hamlet, summoned by Claudius to try to find out what ails him. Hamlet distrusts them and they fail. They accompany Hamlet on a ship bound for England on the orders of Claudius. Their death comes about because of the substitution of their names for Hamlet's in the death warrant from Claudius, which they are carrying to the King of England. They are often played as a gay couple and given foppish or flamboyant costumes and camp mannerisms to get a laugh from the audience. The fact that the couple cannot easily be differentiated (even Claudius cannot tell them apart) and only ever appear on stage together, talking similarly and alternately, adds significantly to the idea of dualism in the play. They are also duplicity personified, as their disloyalty exposes the myth that childhood friendship is a bond for life; fear and profit can override such considerations. They have a functional and thematic role, and add to the black humour of the play by being foils for Hamlet's wit, but are not characterised or individualised. That we do not know whether or not they are reluctant to be there and to follow their orders adds to the play's large number of unknowns.

Fortinbras

Fortinbras, whose name means 'strong-armed', is an ambitious and effective leader of an army. He is nephew to the present King of Norway, and son of the previous king who was killed in a duel with Hamlet's father. Like Hamlet, he did not succeed to the throne after his father's death. He embodies the external threat of the political and territorial aims of a neighbouring country to Denmark, and has a personal commitment to the profession of soldier and the ideal of military honour. He becomes King of Denmark at the close of the play.

Osrick

As a younger version and double of Polonius, he shows that courtiers and sycophants go together, and illustrates the degree of corruption at the heart of Denmark. He is a foolish foil for Hamlet's word-play, and the butt of his contempt for followers and tools of Claudius. A go-between to arrange the duel is necessary, but this part has often been cut out of performances.

The First Player

A personification of the **theme** of acting, he is important for the plot function of the performance of the Mousetrap. Hamlet identifies with this artiste and word-monger, who is such a contrast to the political intriguers at court. His ability to pretend convincing emotion is a cause of reflection for Hamlet and the audience; it contributes to the appearance versus reality issue, and the questioning of the value of words and passions. A thematic and dramatic level of the play is missing if there are no Players or play within a play.

Marcellus and Barnardo

Though only present in the first act, they are important in being Danes, Christians, and common soldiers performing their duty. Because they are not part of the close inner circle of the court their views or claims are not suspect. They set the scene and atmosphere in preparation for the appearance of the Ghost, and their reaction to it can be taken to be typical of the attitude of the time, in contrast to Hamlet's more complex one.

The Clowns

The dialogue between the pair of locals in the graveyard conveys the common perception of the corruption of the court and class system, and the doubt about the cause of Ophelia's death, thereby contributing to several **themes**. The ability of the first gravedigger to parody legal speech and handle language wittily and perceptively begs various questions about status and intelligence. The comic interlude they provide is in ironic juxtaposition to what has gone before, what is about to occur, and to the job they are engaged in. The hurling around of skulls shows the effect of custom upon feeling, another of the play's themes, and the digging of a hole in the earth contributes to its recurring **imagery** pattern. Hamlet's engagement with the first Clown in repartee is thematically relevant, as well as showing us the common touch of Hamlet in relation to his people, hitherto not demonstrated, and their view of him. Since they do not recognise him, there is a further **dramatic irony**, though they are in another sense the only ones who do recognise the ultimate truth of human destiny on a daily basis: all humans must die, return to the earth from whence they came, and rot.

Heaven, earth and hell

Hamlet is considered to be more Christian than other Shakespeare plays, and directly concerns itself with the life to come and one's preparation for it. Being seasoned for one's passage meant being in a state of grace, i.e. having confessed and repented one's sins and having received forgiveness for transgression through prayer

and from the victim of one's crimes or sins (not distinguishable in a society where all law was church law).

The play works visually and conceptually on three levels, with characters and events associated with each. Medieval and Renaissance paintings, and the Elizabethan stage (with its balcony and trap door), represented heaven as being up, hell as down, and earth as in between. According to the book of Genesis, Adam and Eve were placed on earth, a midway point between heaven and hell created especially for them, and given the free will to choose between them. Paintings of the Day of Judgement depict bodies rising from their graves to ascend to heaven to join the angels or being hurled down to a burning pit full of devils. Movement between the levels, rising and falling, is also characteristic of the play, as are laments concerning lack of movement, being imprisoned and unable to attain the higher level, to reach the golden roof 'fretted with fire'. Claudius aims his prayers upwards but his 'thoughts remain below'; the Ghost was thought to be in heaven but has emerged from the bowels of the earth. Gertrude and Ophelia fall in Hamlet's estimation (and the latter physically falls to her death), as do Rosencrantz and Guildenstern. Hamlet tells Claudius to go and seek Polonius in hell. He sees human nature generally as fallen, and he tries to resist the downward pull exerted on himself during the play. His treatment by Fortinbras at the end of the play can be seen as a **symbolic** raising of Hamlet in tribute to his heroic stature.

Th'other place

Heaven, earth and hell are referred to and linked in other ways in the play. As in the medieval morality plays, Hamlet is **Everyman** and is exercised by whether he and others will rise to heaven or be dragged down to hell. We are all 'indifferent children of the earth' 'crawling between heaven and earth'; a 'quintessence of dust' but with 'the apprehension of angels'. The language of the play consistently refers to an afterlife and its physical location. Hamlet's noble father, previously believed to be in heaven, has been reduced to 'this fellow in the cellarage'. Hamlet would like to think of his father as a god, a Hyperion or a Hercules, but has been made brutally aware that he is a 'mole' constrained below the earth; he comes to see mankind as nothing better than a diet for worms. The verb 'fall' is used many times in the play, and the general recurring movement is from high to low, as in all **tragedy**, as the mighty become physically and **metaphorically** fallen. As a representative of the heavy element earth, associated with melancholy, Hamlet feels the downward pull towards his father and his own grave from the start of the play, when his gaze is lowered to the dust and the baser elements in human nature appear dominant all around him. He feels imprisoned in rotten Denmark and burdened by his own solid and sullied flesh. However, he also aspires to a higher ideal, and thus becomes a battleground for opposing elements — fire and air (light and heavenly) versus water and earth (heavy and hellish) — and in his mind the *psychomachia* of the human condition is taking place.

The life to come

Hamlet, Claudius and Laertes each refer to their spiritual state and the afterlife — of which the Ghost is a walking **symbol** — but in rather different ways. Only Hamlet has a 'conscience' which restrains his actions because of the fear of the consequences in the next life. Hamlet is horrified by what happened to his father and is concerned for his own soul and those of his mother and Ophelia; he feels it his duty to try to steer the two women towards salvation. Neither woman expresses any independent concern about the state of her soul; and this is consistent with the misogynistic view that women were lower creatures unable to fully appreciate spiritual matters without male guidance. The reason Hamlet gives for not killing Claudius at prayer is that he is 'fit and seasoned for his passage' (III.3.86) and would therefore go to heaven. This is not at all Hamlet's intention, since old Hamlet was murdered 'with all [his] imperfections on [his] head' (I.5.79) and Claudius is therefore responsible for his being punished in purgatory. Claudius is aware of the need to repent his sins but is unable to do so. He is very conscious in his **soliloquy** in Act III scene 3 of the difference between 'up' and 'down', 'above' and 'below', and that different rules apply in this life and the next. Knowing better but choosing worse was considered more culpable than ignorance. Laertes in his wrath says that he dares damnation, and would even consider committing murder in a church. However, Hamlet and Laertes exchange forgiveness for each other's deaths, which was considered necessary for a passage to heaven.

Suicide was believed to lead to automatic damnation and excommunication, hence the problem with Ophelia's burial rites, her death being 'doubtful' (V.I.223). That Horatio offers to commit suicide for Hamlet is therefore even more generous an offer than it seems, since he is not only willing to lose his life for his friend's sake, but also his immortal soul.

Obsession with death

Hamlet is unusual in having a total of nine deaths, on and off stage, before or during the action of the play, including that of old Hamlet (but not old Fortinbras). All the deaths in the play are violent or unnatural. There are many different types and causes of death referred to: murder, single combat, battle, suicide, beheading, stabbing, poison (various), drowning. Critics have concluded that the play has an obsession with death.

The play begins with references to a death and a funeral, contains further deaths and funerals, and ends with a stage littered with bodies as befitting a battlefield. It is a dark play, being set at night, and with 'sable' (the heraldic colour black), the

colour of melancholy, as Hamlet's adopted colour since he is in mourning. Much of the dialogue and the soliloquies refer to death and beyond. War, duels, and madness are all pertinent to the **theme** of death, as is the frequent use of the word itself (and the related ones of 'grave', 'earth' and 'poison'), and also the presence of skulls, the traditional *memento mori*. The combined and dominant effect of the **imagery** and stage action — in which so many characters are literally laid low — is of Hamlet being a man selected and claimed for death the moment the Ghost beckons him away from the others (who survive), and of the play being the process of his coming to accept his mortality, his place beside his father and Yorick in the earth of the graveyard of Elsinore. Born on the day that the grave-digger began his occupation, Hamlet has lived all his life under death's shadow. As inevitable in a **tragedy**, death features strongly in the play; but since there are more deaths of individuals in *Hamlet* than in other Shakespeare tragedies it could be argued that death is itself a theme. It is the one sure thing in an unsure world, and therefore it is necessarily central to a play about human existence.

Memory and the afterlife

Hamlet feels that his mother and uncle have done his father a grave disservice in cutting short the mourning period and holding a wedding celebration, as the rejection of old Hamlet's memory is tantamount to a refusal to let him live on in the minds of the people. They also try to expunge Hamlet's memories of his father, whereas the Ghost begs him to 'Remember me'. Hamlet is adamant that Horatio should live to tell his own tale, and ensure that his memory lives on appropriately, as near to the truth as can be. Other memories are deliberately untruthful: Gertrude turns Ophelia's doubtful death into a Romantic story, poetic in its imagery and **pathos**; the Players turn history into myth, exaggerating for dramatic effect. The despised characters in the play, notably Claudius, Polonius, Rosencrantz and Guildenstern, those who have betrayed love and friendship through cowardice and self-serving, will not be remembered well. Life and glory is ephemeral for everyone, so the only way in which a saint or hero can be immortalised is in the remembering through the retelling.

Though Catholics believe in purgatory and believe that prayers for the dead ameliorate their condition in the afterlife, the Reformation denied the existence of purgatory and banned memorial masses for the dead. This means that for the Protestant Prince Hamlet — apparently haunted by a Catholic ghost — his options for showing respect for the memory of his departed father are either dutiful revenge or mythologising his attributes.

Providence

There are different terms used for the controlling divine agent in the play: God, He, fate, gods, heaven, destiny, divinity, the almighty, the Everlasting, providence, chance.

Because of the Lord Chamberlain's censorship of blasphemy in the theatre the references to God which could be made on stage at this time were very limited. In other plays, for example *King Lear*, Shakespeare avoids mentioning a specifically Christian deity (although Cordelia represents Christian virtues), instead referring vaguely to 'the gods' as classical literature does. Providence, by definition, was benevolent, providing for humans; whereas fate is a pagan idea and, like destiny, could be malign or random. The two are not, however, distinguished in *Hamlet*, and in this play a single deity is appealed to by a host of titles. Hamlet believes on the one hand that he was born to set right the problem of an out-of-joint Denmark, but he is also tortured by the idea that he must use his own judgement and be responsible for finding his own way out of the moral maze he is in. The traditional **paradox** (and one that much exercised John Milton in *Paradise Lost*) is that an omniscient God has foreknowledge but the individual has free will. By the time Hamlet fittingly appears in the graveyard at the beginning of Act V, however, the apparent conflict has been resolved; he accepts that his destiny has been predetermined and sanctioned by a Christian deity, that even the fall of a sparrow is part of the divine plan, and that there is no need for further questioning and conscience-searching. Apparent randomness is under the control of providence; even Hercules could not change fate. Hamlet is now resolved to follow Horatio's early advice — as shown in the comments 'Let it work' (III.4.206) and 'Let be' (V.2.218) — and allow heaven to direct events, without compromise to his soul. In this way, by being receptive to the signs sent to show him the way and by regarding coincidence as 'sweet' and not random, he becomes an agent of divine retribution. Father's command and God's will are now one and the same.

Coincidence

Coincidence, literally meaning two things coming together, is part of the pattern of doubling in the play, like the ironic coupling of a funeral with a wedding. There are coincidences in the play, where 'two crafts directly meet', which are suggestive of heaven's ordinance rather than blind chance: the arrival of the Players, a key pivot to the plot, is fortuitous; the pirate intervention could not have been foreseen by anyone, and they take only Hamlet and return him to Denmark — and how convenient that Hamlet has his father's signet ring with him, without which he could not have switched the letters and hoist Rosencrantz and Guildenstern with their own petard; the opportune arrival of Fortinbras and his army at the end of the play smacks of good timing and design. Other chance meetings are Hamlet with Fortinbras's army marching to Poland, and Hamlet choosing to visit the graveyard just before the arrival of Ophelia's funeral procession. It seems further confirmation of the guiding role of fate that it is the skull of Yorick, Hamlet's childhood friend, which is thrown up in the graveyard, out of Ophelia's grave. Like all the interruptions in the play, of which there is at least one in every scene, coincidences are proof

of human powerlessness to control events and outcomes and that 'There's a divinity that shapes our ends' (V.2.10).

Perennial questions

The following questions are always asked since there is reason for doubt and conflicting evidence in each case, and the answer makes a difference to our perception and evaluation of an aspect of the play.

How old is Hamlet?

Hamlet is often considered to be the epitome of adolescent angst and is frequently played by a young actor. This means that his mother can still be relatively young and attractive, given that noblewomen were usually mothers by their mid-teens (like Juliet's mother in *Romeo and Juliet*, Juliet is married at 14). Ophelia's lament on the loss and waste of Hamlet being 'Blasted with ecstasy' in III.1.161 mentions his youth, and their relationship generally seems to be one of young and inexperienced love. He wants to continue his studies at Wittenberg, fuelling the idea of a young student prince. The Ghost addresses him as 'thou noble youth' and Polonius tells Ophelia not to trust him because 'he is young'.

However, Act V scene 1 makes him middle-aged for the period; the gravedigger claims to have been in his sexton's job 30 years and to have begun it the 'very day that young Hamlet was born' (l. 145). Yorick, who used to carry him on his back, has been dead for 23 years, which is consistent with Hamlet now being 30. European male royalty, having no duties until called upon to rule, often remained students for their whole lives, and in any case there is no direct evidence that Hamlet is a student at Wittenberg currently. A. C. Bradley is firmly of the opinion that he is not, and interprets his desire to go back there as symptomatic of his melancholy desire to escape from the prison of Denmark and regress to an earlier period of his life when he was happy. Hamlet has more reason to feel aggrieved at Claudius having 'Popped in between th'election and [his] hopes' (V.2.65) if he has reached a mature age. However, this would make Gertrude at least 44, which would make her very old by Elizabethan standards, and not only more deserving of Hamlet's censure of her sexual appetite but unlikely to have the sexual allure necessary to explain Claudius's obsession with her. The age of Hamlet's friends and schoolfellows is also dependent upon his age, and we do not know how long it is since Hamlet has been in contact with Laertes, Horatio, Rosencrantz and Guildenstern, although this would affect our view of his relationships with them.

It has been suggested that 30 years was a round number which was used to denote a serious length of time, a passing of a generation, and was not meant to be taken literally, in which case Hamlet may be no more than 20. This theory is supported by the number 30 being used in the *Murder of Gonzago* as the length of time the King and Queen have been married, although that figure may be deliberate if it happens to be the true one for old Hamlet and Gertrude and the age of Hamlet. There is no direct correlation in Shakespeare between character traits and numerical age; for example, it is hard to believe that the bitter and jaded Iago is only 28, or that the immature Othello is in his forties. The point is that in meeting the gravedigger, who reminds Hamlet of his childhood, Hamlet has come to the end of his life span, has completed the journey from cradle to grave. And though nothing like 10 years have passed during the course of the play, he is older and wiser and even more world-weary than the Hamlet we first see, the one who recently wrote naive love poetry free of doubts, before being 'shocked into complexity' (Shapiro p. 334). Hamlet's double age is consistent with the play being inconsistent, and fits the two sides of his character: reflective yet impetuous, cynical and idealistic.

Who is Horatio and what is he doing there?

It seems odd that we need to ask this question; but it is odd that Hamlet needs to ask Horatio what he is doing in Elsinore, since he has been there at least a month and they both attended the funeral. There has therefore been some critical debate as to whether he is only a visitor to or a denizen of Elsinore, given Hamlet's greeting in I.2.160–61, which is not even clearly consistent with his being a close friend. It is also not clear to the audience why he was on watch with the soldiers in the first scene. Neither Rosencrantz nor Guildenstern show any recognition of him, which is inexplicable if he is a fellow Dane, and Hamlet feels the need to explain to him who Laertes is in the graveyard scene. He knows the military history of 'Our last King', but only saw him 'once'; he is admitted to an audience with Gertrude to give her advice about Ophelia (IV.5), which implies that he is well known in the court circle, but Claudius appears not to have noticed his presence all this time, let alone shown the suspicion of Hamlet's close friend and presumed ally which we would expect. Even stranger, Hamlet tells him 'no revenue hast but thy good spirits/To feed and clothe thee' (III.2.68–69). So what is a pauper doing in the palace and how did he and Hamlet ever become friends?

Perhaps it is because Horatio is not Hamlet's equal — he addresses Hamlet as 'my lord' and generally only speaks when spoken to — and because the funeral would have been crowded, and because Hamlet has understandably been withdrawn and unsociable of late, that this is the first time Horatio has approached Hamlet since he arrived. He is driven to do so by his need to convey the news of the Ghost (though odd that he has not also felt the need to convey his condolences to his friend on the death of his father).

What matters is that the appearance of Horatio in Hamlet's life seems a counterbalance to that of the Ghost and of his false friends. Horatio is uniquely loyal to

the isolated and traumatised prince, and learns to see what Hamlet sees, and by the end wants to go where he is going.

Does Gertrude's affair with Claudius predate old Hamlet's murder?

In the **sources** it did, and this is supported by Hamlet's use of the adjective 'adulterous' when describing his uncle and by his claims that Claudius has 'whored' his mother (V.2.64) and that Gertrude has been false to her marriage vows (III.4.45–46). It would not be adultery if the relationship had begun after the death of her husband, but Hamlet may be exaggerating again. Although a woman's marriage to her ex-husband's brother was of dubious legality, it was not 'incestuous' in the true meaning of the word; yet Hamlet uses this accusation four times in the play (a Freudian slip according to the psychoanalytical, Oedipal critique). If she was unfaithful to her first husband while he lived it makes the case against her much worse in her son's eyes, and reduces audience sympathy for her, although it removes her as the chief motive for the murder, since Claudius was enjoying her favours anyway and did not therefore need to remove his brother on her account. It would make the case against him worse too, as it would suggest that he was not satisfied with cuckolding his brother but wanted his throne as well, and saw Gertrude and Denmark as part of the same deal; having won one he felt entitled to the other. The Ghost, however, also calls Claudius 'incestuous…adulterate beast' (I.5.42) and Gertrude 'seeming-virtuous' (I.5.46), which would seem to be more objective evidence for her affair with his brother while he was still alive. If Gertrude did not simply replace one husband/brother with another, but chose between them while they were alive, it makes sense of Hamlet's presentation of the two portraits in the closet scene and his condemnation of her choice. Furthermore, Hamlet already knew about his mother's remarriage before the encounter with the Ghost, so there must be some new revelation of her wickedness to cause his increased revulsion of his mother during this scene. But the jury is still out (see notes in the Arden edition, p. 214).

Does Hamlet really love Ophelia, and for how long have they been having a relationship?

The evidence that Hamlet does love Ophelia is that he says so in his letters to her, and once to her face, and to Laertes at her funeral. At the end of his fourth **soliloquy** he says to himself 'Soft you now,/The fair Ophelia!' (III.1.88–89) before addressing her, which the audience will believe to be his real feeling towards her unless the words are delivered with sarcasm. His strange way of showing his love may be explained by either the shock and horror of the Ghost's revelations about his mother in particular and women in general; his feeling of obligation to his father that he must wipe from his memory 'all trivial fond records' (I.5.99) out of respect and to keep himself focused on his task; or that he fears for her as a pawn of her father in a corrupt court and hopes that his hostility will drive her to a nunnery and safety. This still leaves the question of when he wrote his love letters to her and first declared his love. If it was before he left for Wittenberg, then their relationship is a long-standing one, as Gertrude's knowledge of it seems to support; yet Ophelia and her father talk of private audiences and tenders of affection that they have given each other 'of late', which would mean that he began their relationship after the death and funeral of his father, which seems most unlikely, given Hamlet's melancholy state of mind since those events. Perhaps Hamlet returned to Elsinore before the death of his father and their affair began then (tying in with Bradley's theory that it is a long time since Hamlet was a student at Wittenberg); but that would make Hamlet present at court when his father died and Claudius took over the throne, raising a whole new set of questions.

What is the question Hamlet is asking in his fourth soliloquy?

The following interpretations are offered by the editors of the Arden edition (p. 485), who favour the first one:

1 He is comparing the advantages and disadvantages of being alive and only tangentially recognising that man has the power to escape a painful existence by committing suicide.
2 The 'question' concerns the abstract choice between life and death and focuses on suicide throughout, but as a concept only.
3 Hamlet is debating whether to end his own life.
4 The question is whether or not Hamlet should kill Claudius.
5 Hamlet is persuading himself that he wishes to proceed with revenge and that he must not let thought interfere.
6 The speech is asking whether one should act or not act as a general principle and practice.

Which lines did Hamlet add to *The Murder of Gonzago*?

Hamlet makes a point of telling the First Player and the audience that he will be adding 'some dozen or sixteen lines' to the playscript of the Mousetrap play but makes no further reference to them. Traditionally the Lucianus lines (III.2.264–69) have been attributed to Hamlet. However, this is not 'sixteen lines' or even a 'dozen', and they seem uncharacteristically crude. It is arguably more likely that he would identify with the First Player/his father and a plausible candidate for the insertion is the section from lines 198 to 223 of the Player King's speech. This is roughly the right length, is less stilted than the surrounding text, and its language contains Hamlet-like doubles, **imagery**, and **themes** ('purpose', 'memory', 'fall', 'passion', 'grief', 'enactures', 'question', 'prove', 'fortune', 'great man down', 'friend', 'enemy', 'overthrown'). The final sentiment of this section — 'Our wills and fates do so contrary run/That our devices still are overthrown' — seems

remarkably coincidental with a recurring preoccupation of Hamlet, as do the lines 'What to ourselves in passion we propose,/The passion ending, doth the purpose lose'. The last couplet of the speech links seamlessly with the first, supporting the belief that the intervening lines are a digression.

Did Ophelia commit suicide?

Although Gertrude says 'an envious sliver' caused the fall into the water and death of Ophelia, the priest says 'Her death was doubtful' (V.1.223). Though she may have fallen accidentally, her lack of attempt to save herself from being dragged down by waterlogged clothing cannot be explained simply by her madness. From the church's point of view she committed suicide because at the least she allowed herself to drown. But as debated by the First Clown/gravedigger and the play as a whole, what constitutes an act or action, and how essential is the element of consciousness? Ophelia in her last utterance in the play sings 'Go to thy deathbed' (IV.5.193) and then does so herself, which raises the possibility of deliberate intent. A further question is: Who watched Ophelia drown? Paintings of the death of Ophelia often have one or more observers in the picture (in keeping with the play's pattern of internal spectators). There must have been an eyewitness for the death to have been reported to Gertrude in such detail (even allowing for her having embellished and romanticised the narrative to create **pathos**), but why did this person or persons not rescue her, a girl fallen into a brook where she floated 'awhile', singing? Not attempting to prevent someone from committing suicide was a mortal sin at that time, and until much later (consider Stephen Blackpool's dilemma in Dickens's *Hard Times*). Would the audience have more or less sympathy for Ophelia if it knew that she had opted out of her life as opposed to just being overwhelmed by it in a mental breakdown?

Why does Fortinbras come to Elsinore?

Does Fortinbras intend all along to break his oath to Denmark and his uncle in order to get revenge for the death of his father in single combat with old Hamlet and to reclaim the lands lost by Norway? In his first speech Claudius admits that Fortinbras has a low opinion of him as the new king, believes 'Our state to be disjoint and out of frame' (I.2.20), and is ready to press his advantage. The Branagh film emphasises Fortinbras's violent intentions on his uninvited and unexpected arrival at Elsinore, which is before he learns of the death of Claudius and Hamlet and therefore that the Danish throne is vacant. Hamlet and Horatio are suspicious, the former asking 'What warlike noise is this?' (V.2.343), and the latter 'Why does the drum come hither?' (l. 355). The military action returns the play to the atmosphere of war between the two nations with which it began and within which the domestic mayhem has been an interlude. This point is emphasised in the Branagh film, which ends with the Norwegian army invading Elsinore and destroying the palace and statue of old Hamlet. One gets the feeling that Fortinbras has not called by to give his respects to Claudius, and that he would have seized the throne anyway, without Hamlet's 'dying voice'. It is consistent with the duplicity of all the characters in the play except Horatio that Fortinbras should be as untrustworthy as he is ambitious, but it makes it ironic that Hamlet should nominate as new King of Denmark someone who gave his word and broke it. It shows, however, how the evil within one man, Claudius, has spread to the point of causing the downfall of the state, since it is implied that Fortinbras would not have come to seize power if Hamlet had been put on the throne.

Interruptions, 'indirections' and delays

It is made abundantly clear in the play that intentions are a form of **hubris**, since a higher power than humans governs their affairs, thwarts their intentions and shapes their ends. A combination of interruptions, deflections and delays mean that purposes are 'mistook', 'currents turn awry', and plots double back on themselves like boomerangs, or returned arrows, producing both **irony** and **poetic justice**. Shakespeare had tragic personal knowledge of human failure to determine outcomes, since his only son Ham–let would not be continuing the family line or bearing the newly acquired Shakespeare coat of arms which Shakespeare helped his father to obtain.

The time scheme

One must make allowance for Hamlet's subjective calculations of the passing of time because he feels strongly that an insufficient mourning period has elapsed since his father's death. The actual time frame of the play is between 5 and 6 months (one early critic worked it out as exactly 5 months and 12 days), between winter and early summer judging by the seasonal references. It starts approximately 6 weeks after the funeral and 2 weeks after the wedding, which was 'a little month' later. By the time of the visit of the Players it is 4 months since old Hamlet's death ('nay 'tis twice two months my lord'), by which time Rosencrantz and Guildenstern have been sent for and have arrived, the ambassadors have returned from Norway, and Laertes is established back in Paris. Another month or so must be allowed for Hamlet's abortive voyage to England and return, along with that of Laertes from Paris in response to the news of his father's death. Because of all the journeys and to-ing and fro-ing of characters involved in the plot, the repetitiousness of events, the many and lengthy **soliloquies**, and the chiding of Hamlet by the Ghost for tardiness, the audience has the impression that events are moving slowly and that an inordinate amount of time has passed during the first four acts. This is compounded by planned events being

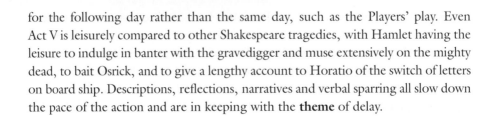

for the following day rather than the same day, such as the Players' play. Even Act V is leisurely compared to other Shakespeare tragedies, with Hamlet having the leisure to indulge in banter with the gravedigger and muse extensively on the mighty dead, to bait Osrick, and to give a lengthy account to Horatio of the switch of letters on board ship. Descriptions, reflections, narratives and verbal sparring all slow down the pace of the action and are in keeping with the **theme** of delay.

'Currents turn awry'

The words 'purpose' and 'intent' are much used, but most plans made in the play fail to achieve their goal. Hamlet is not permitted to return to Wittenberg (since Claudius and Gertrude think for different reasons that it would be better for him to remain with them) and Laertes's return to Paris is very brief. Polonius's plan to eavesdrop on Hamlet in Gertrude's closet goes very wrong for him, and the earlier eavesdropping on Hamlet and Ophelia (whether Hamlet was aware of his and Claudius's presence or not) did not produce anything useful and may have made Hamlet more angry and suspicious. Polonius could not have caused his daughter more harm if he had tried, although he was allegedly protecting her and thinking of her welfare when he interfered in her relationship with Hamlet. Claudius's aiming of Hamlet towards exile — 'everything is bent/For England' (IV.3.44–45) — and a discreet execution is a conspicuous failure, as is the attempt by Rosencrantz and Guildenstern to sound Hamlet out. Laertes's careful preparations for the duel backfire on himself, as well as on his co-conspirator Claudius, and also destroy Gertrude, none of which was intended. She once had hopes that Hamlet would marry Ophelia, as presumably did Ophelia. The Ghost presumably did not intend the death of his ex-wife or of his son when he ordered Hamlet to carry out revenge on his behalf. Hamlet's plans possibly fare better; the Mousetrap plot achieves the intended outcome of getting Claudius to reveal himself (though he has the fortuitous arrival of the Players to thank for this otherwise impossible test), and it could be said that Hamlet does carry out his intention, ultimately and by a very roundabout route, to kill Claudius and avenge his father; but he does not actually plan it himself. If Fortinbras intended to seize the throne of Denmark he is successful, but not in a way he could have imagined.

'Abatements and delays'

Delay is associated with hesitation and therefore doubt. From beginning to end the play contains false starts. The first scene creates an expectation which is not satisfied since the Ghost refuses to speak on its first three appearances and the scene has to be re-run the following night. Given that old Hamlet has been dead for about 6 weeks, there has already been an unconscionable delay in his decision to seek revenge through Hamlet. Hamlet's delay in drinking the wine prepared by Claudius causes his mother's death. There are many other examples of delay between the first and last scenes, including that of Claudius in realising that Hamlet is his enemy, and of Gertrude in realising that her new husband is not a nice man. Delay builds tension and mistrust — the Ghost doubts Hamlet because he defers the acting out of his 'dread command' — and it also gives opportunity for changing of mind and for scheming, as well as irony. If Laertes had not been persuaded to delay his demand for instant satisfaction for the death of his father he would have killed Claudius and his followers would have made him King of Denmark.

Delay works both ways, however, giving time to reflect, to become reconciled to inevitabilities, and to remain free in body and soul. 'The interim is mine' says Hamlet (V.2.73), intending to make use of the delay before the ambassadors can come from England with the news which would give Claudius the excuse to imprison Hamlet, or worse. Their arrival only 20 lines after the killing of Claudius shows how narrowly Hamlet succeeded in his task, which would otherwise have been terminally interrupted. Purposes are more likely to be mistook if carried out hastily, as Hamlet learns from his murder of Polonius. Also, lack of delay, such as that between old Hamlet's death and Gertrude's 'o'erhasty marriage', the funeral and the wedding feasts, is unseemly; his father's memory has not been given its due period of respect. Hamlet is in a sense living on borrowed time from the moment he meets his father's ghost. As he comes to realise, 'The readiness is all' and whether something is now or to come is no matter: 'it will come' (V.2.216). The truth will out, 'foul deeds will rise', and there will be a reckoning sooner or later.

Interruptions

An interruption is a deflection of an intention. The majority of conversations, speeches and actions in the play suffer interruption of one form or another: the funeral of old Hamlet was an interruption in the lives of Hamlet and Laertes, who were called back from Wittenberg and Paris respectively; the Mousetrap perform-ance is not completed; Hamlet's voyage to England is intercepted; Laertes returns from Paris before Reynaldo can report on him, and the commissioner of the report dies before he can receive it; in Act IV scene 7 Claudius is interrupted as he is presumably about to tell Laertes of his England plot. Many characters are lacking important information because of these interruptions. From first to last, speeches are curtailed and never completed because of the unexpected arrival of another character, from the Ghost in Act I scene 1 to Fortinbras in Act V scene 2; and even Hamlet's dying words do not complete the sense or sentence he embarked upon. This characteristic not only adds tension to the dialogue and situation, but it has the additional effect of drawing attention to the limitations of human control as conveyed by the unfinished interactions. The soliloquies could also be seen as a form of interruption of the action.

Images of deflection

Indirection and failing to reach the target are concepts built into the **imagery** of the play.

There are many phrases used to denote an indirect approach, physically or **metaphorically**, to people and problems: 'this encompassment and drift of question'; 'currents turn awry'; 'by indirections find directions out'; 'hoist with his own petar'; 'there's a divinity that shapes our ends'; 'return to plague the inventor'; 'windlasses and assays of bias'. Act V scene 2 uses the sailing metaphor of yawing, which describes the motion of a ship that fails to keep a straight course; 'The time is out of joint' is a bone-setting metaphor, meaning things are unnatural and out of true alignment. As the Scots poet Burns said, 'The best-laid schemes o' mice an' men/Gang aft agley' ('oft go awry'), and this is the message that is built into the language and plot of the play: the Ghost views Hamlet's verbal attack on Gertrude as a deflection of purpose; Claudius intends to pray but fails; Polonius adopts an indirect means of discovering information about his son in Paris. There are also roundabout routes to the destinations of journeys; Fortinbras sets off from Norway to arrive in Denmark by way of Poland; and metaphorically Hamlet's route to revenge and the killing of Claudius could be described as indirect, and a result of divine intention rather than his own.

Arrow imagery is used to convey the deflection and falling short of human intention and metaphorical or actual aiming, shooting and killing. Not only are targets not reached, but the missile doubles back on the sender in a satisfyingly ironic and just way when arrows revert to their bow. Hamlet uses an arrow image when he talks of the 'shot and danger of desire' (I.3.35) and 'I have shot my arrow o'er the house/And hurt my brother' (V.2.237–38). His killing of Claudius could be described as indirect, a divine intention rather than his own.

Why does Hamlet delay?

This is the 'problem of problems'; there is no agreement among readers and critics on this question, which has been debated for centuries. Dr Johnson asked in 1765 whether Hamlet was an instrument or an agent, passive or active, since the outcome is achieved by a stratagem which Hamlet had no part in producing. Certainly he differs from Shakespeare's other tragic heroes in having as little responsibility for the conclusion as he does for the crime that set the train of events in motion. On a practical level, there aren't really any previous opportunities for Hamlet to kill Claudius, since a king is protected day and night by his 'Switzers', and Claudius is suspicious of Hamlet from the beginning.

The usual arguments are that it is (a) a question not worth asking because it is a necessary plot device; (b) it shows the difficulty of taking action for rational beings accustomed to thinking everything through and weighing everything up; (c) it distinguishes his character favourably from Laertes, the hot-head who does not bother with facts or calm reflection and thus puts himself into the hands of the scheming Claudius; (d) it is necessary for Hamlet to first be assured that it is divine will, and then he will not have to bear the guilt of and punishment for murder; (e) it provides a large proportion of the irony (e.g. his self-comparison with the First Player) in a play which depends on it.

If what Hamlet is seeking is not revenge but justice — and the two are not the same — then he is right to delay until he has finished testing everyone and everything. Swinburne defends Hamlet's procrastination by saying that if he has trouble making up his mind, it may be because he has 'somewhat more of mind than another man to make up' (Jump, p. 36). Also G. Wilson Knight (Jump, p. 41) suggests that there is a problem about the 'relative morality' of Claudius and Hamlet because of the prayer scene, which makes it no longer as clear-cut to either Hamlet or the audience what Hamlet should be trying to do. Coleridge's explanation is that Hamlet cannot reconcile the real and the imaginary and is living on two levels simultaneously, 'his thoughts, images and fancy being far more vivid in his perceptions, and his very perceptions instantly passing through the medium of his contemplations, and acquiring as they pass a form and colour not naturally their own'. Furthermore, he argues that Hamlet cannot react to circumstances because of his 'aversion to personal, individual concerns, and [need to] escape to generalizations and general reasonings' (Hawkes, p. 176). Ernest Jones's **Oedipus** argument (Lerner, p. 62) is that Hamlet delays because in killing Claudius he would be killing his other self, the one who desires his mother, and that this is why the two have to perish together finally; Hamlet and Claudius have become bonded in antagonism through rival love for Gertrude.

What must be agreed is that finally, despite or because of the delay, he is able to achieve his purposes of saving his mother's soul, meting justice to Claudius, and avenging his father's death. Had he performed the deed earlier, he may have saved his own life, and that of others, but he would not then have been a tragic hero who did not deserve to die. If his fatal flaw — either character weakness or lapse of judgement — was to hesitate, it did not cause the tragedy and only postponed the inevitable, making Hamlet different from other Shakespeare tragic heroes who are allowed to make real choices.

Melancholy, madness and memory

The modern psychological label of manic depression (bipolar disorder) fits Hamlet very well; it was a mental state recognised, if not so called, at the time, and blamed on melancholy caused by excessive introspection. Melancholy (the word means 'black bile') was considered an unnatural state, a physical disease cause by an imbalance between the four elemental fluids or bodily humours composing the human body. Timothy Bright wrote in his contemporary *Treatise of Melancholie* (1586): 'Melancholy blood is thick and gross, and therefore easily floweth not.' It was believed that evil spirits appeared to introverted minds out of touch with reality, and that way lay madness and then damnation. As Henry Mackenzie puts it: 'The melancholy man feels in himself...a sort of double person' (in Jump, p. 25), and a fractured mind was vulnerable to the devil's schemes to entrap human souls.

It was in the tradition of revenge **tragedy** that the aggrieved character should become mad with rage. Madness is a response to two opposing and irreconcilable forces which the mind cannot cope with, an **ambiguity** which it cannot reconcile; it is therefore the temporary or permanent escape from intolerable shock or pressure. A mad person no longer has to feel guilty or responsible for their actions, which, even if they are aware of them, can be attributed to another self (as with Hamlet when excusing himself to Laertes in Act V scene 2). It was believed that moods of madness fluctuated with the weather and wind direction, southerly breezes being the more wholesome to the afflicted mind; hence Hamlet's comment of II.2.377–78. It was also thought that they were affected by the moon's cycle and were especially prevalent and violent at full moon, hence the word 'lunacy'. Fits and remissions in the hero's lunacy were a feature of the **source** play, *The Spanish Tragedy*, also called *Hieronimo's Mad Again*.

Forms of madness in *Hamlet*

Passion was considered to be both a manifestation and a cause of madness, a kind of delirium called an 'ecstasie' (which literally means standing outside oneself), because it meant a loss of control by the rational mind. Ophelia's madness is a classic case of the mind being overloaded with passion (literally 'suffering') and throws into relief Hamlet's method of coping with the similar anguish of grief and betrayal. The name 'Amlodi' in Norse referred to a fool or weak-minded person. On the other hand, the '**divine idiot**', the fool who in his childlike innocence is actually closer to God and has greater insight than ordinary mortals, has a respected place in the history of literature and cinema. It was a particular feature of the medieval **Romance** that sensitive young noblemen were driven mad by unrequited or rejected love. Polonius is certain that this is the cause of Hamlet's lunacy. Grief, however, is an extreme emotion which can present itself as physical or mental breakdown, and Gertrude attributes her son's madness to 'His father's death and our o'erhasty marriage' (II.2.57). Suicide occurs, at least as a discussion topic, in the play, and has been traditionally regarded as evidence of being of unsound mind. A kind of madness or rage is thought to be required by a ruthless warrior in action, as exemplified by Pyrrhus.

Madness also has a comic mask, however, as displayed by Hamlet when playing the fool as the court jester whilst in 'antic disposition' mode. This links with the play's **themes** of performing for an audience and wearing a false face. There are other famous fools in Shakespeare's comedies and tragedies (notably Feste in *Twelfth Night* and King Lear's Fool), who are **paradoxically** the wisest characters in the play; since they are not directly involved in the action and the passion, they can clearly observe and perceptively comment on the state of humanity in general and the immediate situation in particular. Hamlet observes everyone closely and has a 'prophetic soul'. Fools (who wore 'motley', a half-and-half, two-toned costume) were masters of the **pun** and *double entendre* (as self-protection against their employers' taking offence). They were descended from the ancient oracles, who when consulted put themselves into a state of ecstasy before pronouncing their ambiguous verdicts.

Madness, real or affected, disguised a person's thoughts and intentions, and could therefore be a threat to others; Claudius is certain that 'Madness in great ones must not unwatched go' (III.1.189). Eighteenth-century critics criticised Hamlet's madness as an unwise and unsuccessful tactic, since it caused his removal from the court.

Reasons for putting on an 'antic disposition'

The idea is put into Hamlet's head by Horatio in I.4.73–74, and he immediately sees the practical and moral benefits of adopting the role of madman:

- Touchstone, the fool in *As You Like It*, says 'The fool doth think he is wise, but the wise man knows himself to be a fool'. Hamlet accepts the truth of this saying by admitting he is a fool, in contrast to Polonius, who is a real fool but thinks he is wise.
- He is the paradoxical sad clown, donning the theatrical mask of comedy to hide the tragic face beneath, thus representing the dual nature of all things. Hazlitt called Hamlet **oxymoronically** 'the most amiable of misanthropes' (in Jump, p. 30), who can jest while being cast down by the *tristia mundi* (sadness of the world).
- Adopted madness sets him apart from the those who have betrayed him and whom he despises. The other characters rarely address him directly or voluntarily. His isolation makes a statement that he does not wish to be a part of the court of Denmark, or even of the human race.
- It is a regression to childhood and a mark of respect to the deceased and much missed playmate Yorick to take on the vacant role of court jester. It may also be a signal to his mother and new father that if they insist on treating him insultingly as a child he will behave like one; since he is not allowed to be king (or a student, or a lover) he will take the opposite role of the king's fool.
- Edward Dowden said: 'Madness possesses exquisite immunities and privileges. From the safe vantage of unintelligibility [Hamlet] can delight himself by uttering

his whole mind and sending forth his words among the words of others, with their meaning disguised, as he himself must be' (in Jump, p. 76).

- The possession of such a secret as he has sworn to keep makes it impossible for him to behave normally as though nothing has happened, and it would be an insult to his father to attempt to do so. Anything less than changing his life and adopting a different persona would not match up to the extreme situation of having received a visitation from another world of the tormented ghost of his murdered father.

- Paradoxically, it is a reasoned position in an unreasonable world to take up unreason, in order to draw attention to and condemn the unreasonable behaviour of others. The world has turned topsy-turvy, the old certainties, customs, duties and bonds no longer apply, so it is now appropriate for a lover of wisdom (the meaning of 'philosopher') to embrace nonsense.

- It is a necessary escape to adopt unreason when reason becomes unbearable. Adopted madness will preserve him from real madness when he senses that he is on the verge of what would nowadays be called a nervous breakdown. By dividing himself from himself he aims to reduce the psychological damage.

- Madness is a useful disguise to deceive the spying enemy, and by neatly reversing their own method against them he can watch, confuse and test others as they are doing to him. He can get closer and observe more from behind the screen of his madness.

- It is a protective delaying tactic while he embarks on a quest to establish the facts. Playing the fool is a method of 'by indirections find[ing] directions out'. It allows him to absent himself in pursuit of the truth, a mental equivalent of the physical absence of the Duke in *Measure for Measure* and other exiled truth-seekers in Shakespeare.

- It alters his perception of others to be able to elicit responses not normally possible within conventional discourse and relationships. For example, Polonius patronises the mad Hamlet, and the mad Hamlet can be sexually explicit to the women.

- Fools had a licence to say what they pleased with impunity, and were the only people at court allowed to mock 'great ones'. Thus Hamlet can relieve his feelings and attack Claudius and Polonius with his provocative sarcasm and satire. As A. J. A. Waldock puts it, from the shelter of his madness and 'with the security of a jester, he launches his barbs' (Lerner, p. 85). He can unburden himself of opinions that he could not otherwise express: 'Hamlet's madness is made to consist in the full utterance of all the thoughts that had passed through his mind before — in telling home truths' (Hawkes, p. 172).

- It may, albeit subconsciously, be a way of punishing his mother and causing her to feel distress about his state, as well as reminding her that she too should be feeling grief for her ex-husband and Hamlet's father.

T. S. Eliot, however, saw Hamlet's 'antic disposition' as emotional relief, a buffoonery which can find no outlet in action. Waldock (Lerner, p. 84) and other critics are not convinced that Hamlet has any motive for putting on madness, believing that this is material badly assimilated from the original play and that Shakespeare's play suffers irremediably from the delay/madness theme being tacked on to the basic revenge theme.

'This distracted globe'

The theme of satirists has always been that a madman is no madder than anyone else, and is arguably saner, since the true madness is that of the world itself. Madness gives Hamlet an *alter ego* which reinforces the doubleness motif in the play, and which makes him a **microcosm** of out-of-joint Denmark. The poison has spread outwards from Claudius, and everyone he is in contact with becomes corrupted; therefore it is fitting that Hamlet appears to have been infected too. Madness is an actualisation of the **metaphor** of sickness in the play: 'My wit's diseased' (III.2.329–30). It supports the recurring **imagery** of decline and fall, conveyed by the downward movements within the play, that his mind should appear to have been 'o'erthrown'. It adds further doubt for the audience, who cannot be absolutely certain how feigned Hamlet's madness is; some critics claim that he does become truly mad when the mask becomes the reality. Hamlet is already a feeler and a speaker; he becomes an actor when he puts an 'antic disposition on', performing a play within a play even before the Players arrive. He recognises that he is Fortune's fool, and his new role betokens this subjection to the female persona, just as he feels subject to his mother (who deprives him of the throne and of herself, and refuses him leave to return to Germany) and to Ophelia (who returns his love tokens). His moving in and out of madness reflects the shifting nature of an erratic world. Madness disguises truth as the earth hides foul deeds and a smile disguises a villain. Importantly for the variety of the play's language, madness enables him to take on another mode of discourse, one composed of 'wild and whirling' and 'pregnant' words, and snatches of ballads and proverbs, which are all methods of being enigmatic. Since madmen were expected to dress negligently, as Ophelia describes Hamlet's appearance in Act II scene 1, madness provides Hamlet with a costume as well as a language change, an exterior to match the interior abnormality.

Ophelia's madness

Hamlet's supposed madness provides an opposite parallel for Ophelia's genuine madness later. Hers is precipitated by a double grief, for both her father's death and her lover's exile, possibly compounded by the knowledge that her ex-lover is her father's murderer. Women's minds were considered weaker than men's and less able to withstand emotional trauma, not only because they were created with inferior intellects but because they were governed by the inconstant moon (because of

menstruation) and possessed a womb ('hysteria' comes from the Greek for womb), which was thought to be the seat of extreme emotion. When Hamlet leaves, the role of mad person in court becomes vacant again, and her assuming it makes her one of Hamlet's many doubles. Furthermore, both lose their father through violence; both find memory, and the comparison between what was and what is, unbearable; both are imprisoned, isolated and watched; both suffer from the diabolical conspiracy of Claudius and Polonius.

Ophelia's situation is worse than Hamlet's, however, in that having lost her father and been abandoned by her lover, she has no future prospects, and would quite likely have ended up in the nunnery that Hamlet has ordered her to. Ophelia's mad songs unwittingly reveal a side of her which has been unsuspected by the other characters (one too shocking for eighteenth-century theatre-goers), whereas Hamlet uses madness to conceal.

The significance of memory

Memory was regarded as a duty, as it is a mental faculty which distinguishes humans from animals, and is a means of respecting the dead. Hamlet therefore takes exception to Claudius lecturing him on why he should forget his father in Act I scene 2, and to his mother having forgotten his father so quickly. Memory can also be a painful burden, a weighing down of the spirits which induces melancholy. For Hamlet memory is a distinguishing attribute of humanity and a form of respect; 'a beast that wants discourse of reason/Would have mourned longer' (I.2.150–51). It is his mother's and uncle's refusal to remember his father (though Claudius claims 'The memory be green', I.2.2) which causes his resentment against them even before he learns of the murder. Memory is all that remains to link the living and the dead; as Hamlet painfully demonstrates, the body rots. The Ghost begs Hamlet to 'Remember me' (I.5.91). Though it can make us melancholy to remember ('Must I remember?', I.2.143), it is unnatural and reprehensible to attempt to forget, as our consciences then become hardened. This is why Hamlet must force his mother to access her memories, and why in Act I scene 5 Hamlet writes down something he has learned ('That one may smile, and smile, and be a villain', line 108) as an *aide memoire*, since some things must not be forgotten and memory is fallible.

Memory is what distinguishes the sane from the mad; losing one's mind includes losing one's memory. Ophelia is unable to tell what is present and what is past in her muddled utterances, or to remember court etiquette and what are appropriate sentiments to express in public. Custom and tradition cannot exist without memory. Hamlet enjoins Horatio to stay alive in order to tell his story truthfully, an act of remembrance to keep faith with the departed, who are glorified in retrospect as memory exaggerates and exalts virtues of the noble and honourable to the level of the divine, creating gods and heroes of mortals to redeem their flawed existence on earth.

Memory, like everything else human, has its frailty, and is not susceptible to willpower: the emotional memory cannot be sustained, and when the feeling passes the resolve weakens. Proposals made in the heat of the moment, however sincerely meant at the time, do not turn into action and purpose is defeated. The failure of considered human intentions is a cause of regret to Hamlet because it seems to mean that the only actions that can be carried out are the unconsidered and therefore morally dubious ones, exemplified by his stabbing of Polonius. He also believes that memory can be diluted or deflected by distractions, so that to focus single-mindedly on his duty to avenge his father he feels obliged to wipe his memory of everything else. Conversely, words can trigger involuntary memory, and even Claudius is caught out by something said by Polonius at the beginning of Act III scene 1, as well as by the Mousetrap.

The skull of Yorick is the face-to-face ***memento mori*** of the end to which we must all come, however kind or great, and of the fact that the quality of one's life and death — which determine how one is remembered — are all that finally matter. Hamlet does not need reminding of his mortality after the death of his father and the inescapable proof of the afterlife which is brought by the Ghost. This memory influences all his decisions, curbs all his violent intentions, and is the subject of most of his utterances to others and to himself. His Christian 'conscience' gets in the way of his pagan duty, hence his great dilemma. However, as the wise Hugh in Brian Friel's play *Translations* says: 'to remember everything is a form of madness'.

Plays, players and acting

The cast list includes Players, which at the time meant an itinerant group of performers who, in return for hospitality, provided entertainment at courts and grand houses. *Hamlet* is distinctive in not only using the conceits of acting and putting on a show as intrinsic **themes**, but in also containing a play within a play. Shakespeare uses the stage **metaphor** in other plays, such as *As You Like It* and *Macbeth*, but more than any other this play investigates the medium of theatre and the nature of performance, as well as making topical mention of the London theatres and their companies. In Act II scene 2 there are **puns** on their names, Fortune and Globe, in addition to a denunciation of child actors. Extra levels of **irony** in a work that affects to abhor deception and disguise are that Hamlet's own role involves playacting, and it was Shakespeare's own profession.

Acting and action

The round Globe theatre is the setting for the play and the universe in microcosm. The play within the play is the structural centre of *Hamlet*, with a corresponding symmetry either side of it. It also brings together the entwined actions of revenge

and marriage and forces them to a joint crisis. When the Ghost appears to Hamlet after the play and Polonius is killed, the second revenge cycle begins, which reverses the role of Hamlet and turns Laertes into his avenger.

Performing a deed, performing to spectators, pretending, or just taking initiative as opposed to being passive, are all forms of acting in the play. The word 'act' and its derivatives and synonyms are ubiquitous; the words 'play', 'cue', prompted', 'performance', 'audience', 'prologue', 'stage', 'show', trappings' and 'applaud' all contribute to the theatrical image cluster. 'Act' is also a legal term, discussed by the Clowns in Act V scene 1, which relates to the judgement theme of the play and brings up again the question of active versus passive, with the **paradox** of Ophelia being deserving of a Christian burial only if 'she drowned herself in her own defence' (V.1. 6–7). A more general irony is that an actor appears to be the spontaneous author of his words and actions; but they are in fact scripted by someone else, have been rehearsed and reiterated many times, and are therefore false. This is the point Hamlet makes when reflecting on the First Player's acting — 'What's Hecuba to him, or he to her,/That he should weep for her?' (II.2.556–57) — and when he tells his mother that outward shows of grief 'are actions that a man might play' (I.2.84).

The first actor was Satan, disguised as a serpent and deceiving Eve with his wily words, and the Christian church has therefore always found acting suspect and a sign of a lack of integrity (see Jane Austen's *Mansfield Park*, for instance). Theologically, the good have traditionally been passive, patient sufferers (a triple **tautology**), refusers of action and change, and thereby resisters of temptation. Men of action, like Laertes, do not use their protective reason to curb their excesses; they leap (like Macbeth) from thought to deed in a way that endangers their own souls as well as the lives of others. Some critics believe that in his most famous (fourth) **soliloquy** Hamlet is not engaged in resisting the temptation to commit suicide but debating whether to become active, to 'take up arms' and die in action (which he finally does, following the lead given from above when he is returned by pirates to Denmark). An act was defined legally as having three parts: the imagination, the resolution and the perfection. The course of the play is Hamlet's movement through these stages.

Playing a part

Claudius, the showman and demagogue, performs continuously from his first grand entrance in procession onto the stage. His affected and prolix utterances use the royal plural and overuse characters' names in a style which sounds insincere. Though he pretends to care about the welfare of others, it is really self-interest and political expediency he is considering whenever he speaks, even when praying and when at the end Gertrude drops dead and he lies that 'She swounds to see them bleed' (V.2.302).

Gertrude seems to be pretending that the situation at court and within the family is better than it is, as if she prefers to bury her head in the sand. Though she does not know her new mate killed her previous husband, she guesses how Hamlet feels about the 'o'erhasty marriage' but does not attempt to talk to him about it.

Rosencrantz and Guildenstern are forced to play the role of spies, which means everything they say to Hamlet is contrived and duplicitous. They are, as Tom Stoppard shows in his play based on their experience, players in someone else's play.

Polonius is playing a parody of himself, which would be more amusing if it were not that he bears some blame for the marriage and total blame for Ophelia's betrayal of Hamlet. Hamlet awards him the dunce's cap because he plays the fool throughout his short life in the play, whilst fancying himself to be a serious actor. He also appropriates the role of director whenever he gets a chance: he gives instructions to Ophelia and Gertrude on how to play their rendezvous with Hamlet, and to Laertes on how to act his way through Paris and life.

Laertes seems to be overacting at Ophelia's funeral, adopting the actions and speech mode of the stereotypical ranting revenger. This prevents him from coming across as sincere in his grief for his sister, seemingly more incensed by the damage done to his family's honour, or rather his own.

Hamlet's main objection to women is that they are all actors; they paint their faces and 'jig', 'amble' and 'lisp' to deceive men. He believes honour demands that one should 'Suit the action to the word, the word to the action'. The combined effect of all the playacting is that Hamlet and the audience feel that only Horatio stands out as someone who is what he appears to be, has no affectations, and can therefore be trusted.

This play has many would-be kings: old Hamlet still stalks the battlements dressed as a warrior king; Claudius, 'a king of shreds and patches', usurps the royal title; Gertrude is now 'imperial jointress to this warlike state' (1.2.9) and would not give up her regal position; Polonius once played the emperor Julius Caesar, and dies in mistake for 'his better'; the Player King tells the tragic tale of King Priam of Troy and in the Mousetrap represents old Hamlet as Duke Gonzago; Laertes has raised a mob of followers who cry 'Laertes shall be king!'; Hamlet the Dane is a shadow king who 'was likely, had he been put on,/To have proved most royal' (V.2.391–92), is denied the succession but is able to cancel the edicts of Claudius with his father's signet ring and assume the role of King of Denmark for a matter of minutes; Fortinbras, the king-in-waiting, claims his 'rights of memory' in the kingdom and takes over the throne of Denmark.

Hamlet's roles

Hamlet is reluctant to play the role of the stock avenger, which we see in Laertes, or indeed to conform to any stereotype, a concept he abhors and mocks in Polonius and Osrick. Violence of word and deed do not come naturally to his reflective and moral temperament. What he most aspires to, and saw in his father, is a dignified and worthy playing of the role of man. The ideal **Renaissance** man was characterised

by beauty, wit, and swordsmanship; he should be a poet, a soldier, a courtier and a scholar (like Sir Philip Sidney, for example). That Hamlet was viewed as having achieved this pinnacle of excellence we glean from Ophelia's eulogistic speech about him being the 'rose of the fair state' (III.1.153). He refuses to accept that man should give way to his baser instincts — sex, food, drink and sleep — and play the beast, and he criticises Claudius for having done so, thus bringing Denmark into disrepute. He gives up his role as Ophelia's suitor and refuses to play that of son to his uncle; in his view the former is too frivolous for a time and place 'out of joint' and the latter would be an odious betrayal of his father's memory.

A role he does take on is holding a mirror up to nature (e.g. when he gets his mother to see the error of her ways), believing it to be his job to discover and reveal the truth about everyone and everything. He hands over this role to Horatio on the point of death. He thinks heaven has appointed him 'scourge and minister', the contradictory roles of punisher and priest, and that he is responsible for the salvation of others. He is finally an avenger, but not one motivated by a personal vendetta (his father has not been mentioned since the closet scene). He is acting as a divine agent to purge Denmark of evil and restore justice, the job which he recognised was his when he cursed his fate at the end of Act I, and which he finally accepts and performs with grace and, most importantly, without jeopardy to his soul.

Internal audiences

There is not only a play within a play, but there are audiences within the players throughout the actual play. The stage audiences are either in public view (such as when the whole court watches the fencing match) or hidden and invisible to the characters doing the performing (such as Polonius hiding behind the arras). In the Mousetrap scene there is a parallel theatre audience watching a play, and within that Hamlet and Horatio are watching the King's reaction as a member of that audience. The constant element of putting on a performance in *Hamlet* creates uncertainty for the real audience as to whether characters would be saying or doing the same thing if they were aware or not aware of being watched. This is particularly relevant to the nunnery scene, where it isn't clear whether Hamlet does actually know, or at what point he realises, that Polonius and Claudius are eavesdropping on his conversation with Ophelia. Thus the themes of doubling, doubt and spying are made concrete, and an atmosphere of suspicion and treachery reinforced. Intimate scenes which should be private are not allowed to be so, which disturbs propriety at the court of Elsinore and increases our sympathy for Hamlet as a target of contriving.

Characters watching each other often draw the wrong conclusions (e.g. Hamlet's misreading of Claudius at prayer), which puts the theatre audience on its guard as to its own interpretations. It also makes the point that one cannot trust the evidence of one's eyes, since without sufficient knowledge, or as victims of deliberate deception, we cannot be sure of anything.

'The play's the thing'

The Players and their play make a vital contribution to the action and themes of *Hamlet*. Players make use of all human experience in the two modes of comedy and tragedy, and their trade consists of both words and actions. Hamlet's dilemma lies in not knowing which is the more honourable of these contrary forms of expression. His father's legacy is that of a role model for manly military action without asking questions, and Fortinbras also does not 'unpack his heart with words'; at one point Hamlet scorns words as the expression of not only females but prostitutes ('a very drab'). The stoic Horatio, on the other hand, refuses to be a slave to passion, bases his beliefs on hard evidence, and advises 'If [one's] mind dislike anything, obey it' (V.2.211). Hamlet seems to admire both of these characters and their behaviour, but they represent diametrically opposed attitudes to life, and he is torn between action and reflection until he can find a way of reconciling them.

The Players remind Hamlet of the difficulty of assessing honesty, even in a Ghost, since they can produce tears for a fictional character which are not matched by any genuine feeling. Hamlet is struck by the irony of his having real cause for passion but not the ability to express it adequately, so that **paradoxically** the false seems more true than the truth. The Players, like the madness, add to the range of styles in the play and enable sudden shifts to occur between different forms and registers of language. As lowly characters who take on mighty roles of epic grandeur, they also contribute to the movement between high and low.

The connection between the Pyrrhus play and Hamlet's situation is obvious to the real audience, though ironically not to the internal audience: old weak King Priam is brutally slaughtered by a younger, more virulent and more ruthless adversary in the presence of his wife. She, however, reacts as the archetype of the devoted grieving wife and not as how Hamlet believes his mother reacted to the death of her husband. The play *The Murder of Gonzago* functions as a double and parallel to the main plot, and as a test for the 'conscience of the king'. Without it Hamlet would not have got the supporting evidence for the Ghost's accusation. It enables both internal and external audiences to make comparisons between the behaviour and claims of characters in both plays. On a third and ironic **metafictional** level, the actual audience is being reminded that all plays are false theatrical constructs, fictions and illusions, whose deliberate gaps in information and emotive language are intended to manipulate the emotional and cognitive responses of their viewers; they cannot therefore be trusted or used as proof of anything.

Words, words, words

Hamlet has the largest speaking part in the whole Shakespeare canon, which allows him scope to employ disconcerting shifts of style and to cover the full range of registers from the formal to the **colloquial**, the deadly serious to the comically absurd. In a play about replacing the old with the new, set in such a changing political and social period, it is fitting that there should be so many coinages in *Hamlet*, which contains 170 usages of words new to English. In the traditional opposition of genders, women are words and men are deeds. Laertes and Fortinbras personify the masculinity which Hamlet feels he may lack, given his tendency to verbalise, but it is revealing that in II.2.566 Hamlet envies the Player not Pyrrhus, and chides himself for saying nothing rather than for doing nothing. Everyone in the play talks of Hamlet; he is their subject.

Different styles

The language of all Shakespeare's plays, but this one in particular, is permeated by the Bible, the Book of Common Prayer, and the proverbial sayings of his day, thereby covering a range of styles from the most to the least formal. The catechism mode that is evident (e.g. the interrogation of Horatio by Hamlet in Act I scene 2) befits a play that looks critically at the procedures of the church and the law and that is concerned with questions and answers, argument and evidence, definition and identity. Latin and other legal terminology is used, and parodied, in Act V scene 1. The sayings and ballads, including those uttered by Ophelia in her madness, remind us that this is also a play about quintessential male and female experiences, and the way that these are immortalised in folk songs and stories; beneath the veneer of courtly manners — which are in any case being satirised — the characters are no more than ordinary mortals. In addition to the formal written and the colloquial spoken versions of language — **verse** and prose, serious and comic, narrative and descriptive, personal and public — the **genres** include a love poem to Ophelia and a letter to Horatio, all of which combine to create a comprehensive collage of human emotion and expression.

Language features

The text is notable for its word-play; Frank Kermode points out that the language of the play is characteristically that of repetition and 'doubling and **antithetical** phrases', for example 'This spirit, dumb to us, will speak to him' (I.1.172). This helps to create the duality and contradiction which permeate the play. *Hamlet* is 'obsessed with doubles of all kinds, and notably by its use of the figure known as **hendiadys**' (Kermode, p. 101). This is a way of expressing one concept through two linked nouns or adjectives (e.g. 'gross and scope', I.1.68; 'dead waste and middle of the night', I.2.198; 'a nipping and an eager air', I.4.2; 'the pith and marrow of our attribute', I.4.22; 'expectancy and rose of the fair state', III.1.153; 'wild and whirling words', I.5.133; 'enterprises of great pitch and moment', III.1.86; 'My soul is full of discord and dismay', IV.1.45; 'delicate and tender prince', IV.4.48) and suggests uncertainty and division in everything. Hamlet, Laertes and Horatio

all use this device, of which there are 66 instances in the play; meanings thus recede and multiply, preventing reconciliation. These various forms of doubling are a kind of delaying tactic which, by slowing down the play's delivery, allow tension and menace to build up through threats and intentions unrelieved by action.

Likewise the prefix 'con-' merges or locks together pairs of opposites or parallels (e.g. 'conjoined', III.4. 127), and the prefix 're-', meaning again, creates a double (as in 're-word', III.4.144). **Paradoxes** and **oxymorons** form contradictions through 'the conjunction of what is ordinarily disjunct' (Kermode, p. 103); these compressed parallels emphasise the anomaly of the situation and the relationship combinations (e.g. sister/queen and father/uncle) caused by marriage with one's brother's wife.

Hamlet and the play in general favour plural nouns where singular ones would do, and sorrows, doubts, husbands, fathers, friends, ambassadors and spies all come plurally, outnumbering and overwhelming the lone individual.

The interrogative mode

The dialogue of the play contains a striking number of questions. Unanswered questions, and questions answered with other questions, are a disconcerting device to expose human ignorance and insecurity. Questions, by definition, are a quest for truth; all assumptions and traditional beliefs and practices are questioned in the play. The noun and verb forms of 'question' appear repeatedly. The language of the play reflects its prevailing uncertainty; questions are the main mode of Hamlet's own discourse and he gives few answers. (Tom Stoppard's Rosencrantz complains that he asked them 27 questions in ten minutes and answered only three.)

The play begins with the practical and metaphysical question 'Who's there?', a question Hamlet continues to ask on behalf of the audience. He also questions whether objective reality and morality exist, or only subjective and relative versions. If nothing is either good or bad but thinking makes it so, then how can there be such concepts as good and evil? What makes the difference between deliberately planning and executing the cold-blooded murder of a brother (the sin of **Cain**) and an impulsive stabbing of a hidden intruder believed to be someone else deserving of death? The motive is all. The tenor of the play requires as many questions to be asked as possible, and for feelings to be always in doubt. Knowledge has tradition-ally been imparted through questioning, as in the Catholic catechism and Socratic dialogues; Hamlet is taking on the mantle of temporal judge and spiritual inquisitor by adopting the interrogative mode. Many of his interchanges with other characters take the form of a catechism, such as that with Horatio in Act I scene 2 about the Ghost's appearance. Even his statements and exclamations sound like questions, such as 'What a piece of work is man' and 'How all occasions do inform against me'. War creates an atmosphere of distrust, a fear of spies and of not being able to tell friend from foe without interrogation.

Even as a student, it is Hamlet's job to seek answers, to use his ability to reason, the attribute which raises humans above beasts. His **soliloquies** are an extended form of his questioning of his own state and that of humanity and the universe. Ignorance is not innocence, as Gertrude demonstrates. Though we cannot wholly succeed in turning apprehension into comprehension, it is the wanting to know that distinguishes higher beings from lower. The incidence of questions is much reduced after the killing of Polonius. It seems that Hamlet, who began by questioning the meaning of creation, has come to trust in a providence which ordains our lives and shapes our ends. He is able to arrive at a state of acceptance, and peace with himself, whereby he can make the absolute statement 'The readiness is all' (V.2.216), even though he knows it means his death is imminent.

Language abusers

Polonius's speech (e.g. his second farewell to Laertes in Act I scene 3) resounds in **tautology** and received wisdom; both are types of repetition. His prolix pontificating reveals a paucity of matter and clumsiness of style. Old saws and unsubtle commands are a brutish level of utterance below even that of Caliban, and are also apparent in the speech mode of Osrick, a younger Polonius who also affects what Kermode calls 'pompous tediousness' (p. 109) and 'compulsive duplication' (p. 102) (e.g. II.1.61–65 and I.3.70). Polonius also labours his **puns** (e.g. I.3.106–09), much to the annoyance of Hamlet, who mocks the pedestrian 'Very like a whale' (III.2.389). He represents the kind of people found in royal courts, sycophants who do not respect words but use them to curry favour.

Claudius affects the royal plural and formal declarative style to shore up his stolen throne and can hold forth at considerable length with apparent ease, though the content does not bear close scrutiny as it consists of practicalities and self-justification, expressed by his own admission in 'painted' words (III.1.53) and formulaic phrases.

Laertes is not really interested in words and his warning speech to Ophelia (which she takes to be hypocritical) in Act I scene 3 is pompous, sententious and clichéd, like those of his father.

Rosencrantz and Guildenstern give sycophantic set speeches of received wisdom (e.g. III.3. 11–23) which make them seem false and unsympathetic to Hamlet and the audience; whereas Horatio's measured language in Act I scene 1 is poetic and classical, and contains **rhetorical** structures and diction which reveal his self-control as well as his education.

Hamlet's speech characteristics

Hamlet uses 'we' and 'us', but rarely 'I'. This is not the royal plural which Claudius is so fond of, but the philosopher's plural, talking of the human race and drawing general conclusions from the individual and particular case by inductive reasoning.

He sprinkles his speech liberally with the names of Greek gods, mythological and biblical figures, and ancient rulers (e.g. Nemean lion, Vulcan's stithy, Jove, Hercules, Nero, Herod, Niobe, **Cain**, Alexander and Caesar). His living in an imaginative world of heroes and warriors accounts for his finding his fellow humans disappointing and his inclination to overpraise his father.

Hamlet's first words in the play are a **punning** doublet ('kin' and 'kind') and there will be many more, for example 'I eat the air[heir], promise-crammed' (III.2.103–04), a reference to having been fobbed off with an empty promise of the throne in the future. 'Solid', 'conscience', 'mole' and 'act' are other words which Hamlet extracts a double meaning from early on in the play. Kermode describes his speech mode as 'duplicative' (p. 104), making 'division without distinction' (p. 108). Hamlet's careful balancing of words, bringing together opposites and subtly weighing them in **antithesis** (e.g. 'Be thy intents wicked or charitable', I.4.42; 'More honoured in the breach than in the observance', I.4.16), is a characteristic of Hamlet's language throughout. **Oxymorons**, such as 'quintessence of dust' (II.2.308) and 'paragon of animals' (II.2.307) enable him to yoke together opposites to convey the **paradox** which is the human being. **Stichomythia** is another device which he indulges in, and one which draws attention to word-play as combat, a parallel to fencing, and to the relationship between the pen and the sword, the word and the action.

Hamlet can adapt his speech mode to suit his **interlocutor**; when he is satirising the prolixity and pompousness of Osrick, for example, he apes his outlandish vocabulary by using such archaic and pedantic words as 'infusion', 'semblable', 'umbrage' and 'impawned'.

In Act V scene 1 he uses the **colloquial** language of the villagers of Elsinore, including vernacular words for head — 'mazzard', 'sconce' and 'chops' — and is able to converse with ease and in prose with the First Clown, as he does with the First Player, seemingly having an interest in their occupations and a gift for the common touch. His exchanges with Horatio are, on the other hand, almost entirely in **verse**, which suggests a mutual respect that Hamlet refuses to extend to Osrick. Unusually for a Shakespeare hero (Iago is a villain), Hamlet is sarcastic, as in 'Then there's hope a great man's memory may outlive his life half a year' (III.2.140–41). It is his weapon of choice against his adversaries, male and female: 'I prithee take thy fingers from my throat' (V.1.256); 'good mother' (I.2.77).

W. Clemen points out the absence of **hyperbole** in Hamlet's language, especially by comparison with Lear and Othello. He notes that 'Hamlet prefers to keep his language within the scope of reality, indeed, within the everyday world' (in Jump, p. 65) of trades and objects, games and proverbs — things and words recognisable by the common man rather than figurative language with majestic diction and a cosmic dimension. Though critics view him as the intellectual's intellectual, there is nothing obscure about his expression and choice of diction. His trick of pretending

to misunderstand, always taking the other meaning than the one intended by the speaker, shows: his sensitivity to language; his seeing the world in double vision; his contrariness and independence of character; and his mission to expose imprecision of expression in his fellows and mark himself out from them. His intellectual honesty — 'I know not seems' — makes it impossible for him to be pompous or hypocritical; even with Polonius and Claudius he speaks the simple truth, if they wished to hear it. It is in fact his refusal to dissemble which puts him in danger. Claudius admits he is 'free from all contriving' (IV.7.134), which includes verbal posturing.

As Coleridge pointed out (Hawkes, p. 185), Polonius is a 'man of maxims', whereas Hamlet is a man of ideas who uses words in a considered, precise and individual way. While Claudius often uses studied comparisons, in the form of contrived **similes**, Hamlet's imagination fuses perception into **metaphor**, the subtler and more sophisticated relative of simile. Both Polonius and Claudius express the personal through the sententious and general, thereby distancing themselves from the events and persons with their banalities and effusions, whereas Hamlet expresses genuine feelings 'in a language which bears the stamp of a unique and personal experience' (Clemen, in Jump, p. 69). He shows a disposition to fall into rhyming at moments of high emotional tension, such as after the Mousetrap when he is convinced of Claudius's guilt, and at the grave of Ophelia when the realisation hits him that even Alexander the Great and Caesar are reduced to lumps of clay. His first address to the Ghost employs the philosopher's natural mode of splitting hairs, not to be pedantic but to think precisely upon the event and encapsulate it in language, a form of control for someone who feels they have no other.

Hamlet's attitude to words

Hamlet thinks words should not be abused and should match the sentiments they are being used to express, and he savours sounds like a poet. He berates Ophelia — women in general — for nicknaming God's creatures (III.1.145–46), so strongly does he feel the respect due to words and the importance of using them precisely. Words have the power to secure memory: 'meet it is I set it down' (I.5.107). They are the evidence of intelligence, a tool for persuasion, and a bulwark against the bestial. They should be used to encapsulate ideas and feelings, rather than as Polonius uses them, in hollow maxims and axioms. Hamlet is touched by all forms of epic narrative — tragic drama, myths, legends, ballads and proverbs — the **genres** which inspire humans to aspire. Though he places a high value on words at the beginning of the play, as befits a student given to reasoning and discourse, he comes to distrust them because when corrupted they form part of the armoury of disguise, saying one thing and meaning another. Claudius, Polonius, Rosencrantz and Guildenstern, Osric and Laertes at the graveside are all devaluers of words. Hamlet becomes weary of them and more reluctant to speak as the play progresses. His last words are 'The rest is silence', as if to say that words in the end are not enough; they can neither achieve honour nor effect justice (even for lawyers). They do, however, make stories, which function as memories for those who survive us. Through Horatio, Hamlet's words will live on.

Themes

Binary oppositions are reflected in the **themes**, as in other aspects of the play, and one could say that opposition is in itself a main theme. Many of the themes are also woven into the structure and language of the play; doubling, for instance, as represented in characterisation, plot and style by the pairs of characters, repetition of events and use of **hendiadys** respectively. G. Wilson Knight said 'Death is truly the theme of this play'. Several of the other main themes have been dealt with in other sections of the guide.

Opposing pairs

The play is based on the universal dualities of human nature: mind and body, restraint and appetite, reason and passion, god and beast, body and soul, words and deeds, satyr and Hyperion. From these arise other oppositions within life, the universe or nature, which are the subject of many conversations in the play: heaven and hell, good and evil, sin and absolution, salvation and damnation, flesh and conscience, rising and falling, conception and decomposition. The connection between these apparent opposites exercises Hamlet, and he links them in his utterances, for example 'if the sun breed maggots in a dead dog, being a good kissing carrion…' (II.2.181–82). Heaven and hell are opposed from the beginning, where Christmas is juxtaposed with evil spirits walking abroad, and damnation continues to be the alternative to salvation throughout the play. High and low is the fundamental opposition behind these themes. Actions versus words are also in tension in the language and events of the play, and there is the question of their relative status.

Revenge and forgiveness are always incompatible, although revenge and justice may turn out to be the same. The Old Testament dictum 'An eye for an eye, a tooth for a tooth' underpins the practice of summary execution and capital punishment, but is in conflict with Christianity and the commandment 'Thou shalt not kill', and with God's exclusive right to administer vengeance. The Ghost, inconsistently, wants Claudius to be punished on earth but Gertrude left to heaven.

Custom

Characters comment on customs and habits several times in the play. They are perpetuated and reinforced by repetition and the unquestioning observance of tradition and memory. Hamlet criticises Claudius's observance of the custom of heavy drinking and revelry, saying that it would be 'More honoured in the breach than the observance' (I.4.16). On the other hand, he tells his mother 'Assume a virtue, if you have it not' (III.4.161), and then the custom of celibacy will soon become a habit; the mask will become the reality. Moderation and abstinence are noble habits, whereas the indulgence of bestial appetites disgusts the puritanical Hamlet and in his view degrades humanity. Therefore Hamlet seems to suggest that customs are either good or bad, as thinking makes them so, and belong to the general pattern of those aspects of human existence which have opposing sides. Custom can make the unacceptable seem acceptable, or tolerable, and it can therefore have a protective function; Horatio comments on the Clown who 'sings in grave-making' that 'Custom hath made it in him a property of easiness' (V.I.66–68). However, it also encourages unquestioning, repetitive behaviour and has the power to imprison the will.

Imprisonment

A range of diction and situations conveys this theme: 'Mousetrap', 'nutshell', 'between heaven and earth', 'grave'; the multiple use of the word 'confine'; not being allowed to return to Germany; always being spied upon. A feeling of imprisonment was a symptom of melancholy, as was having bad dreams. Hamlet is trapped ('be-netted', V.2.29) in an unwelcome family set-up, between an old and a new order, between natural and supernatural worlds, and is effectively under house arrest. Denmark is a prison in that those who arrive find it difficult to leave, except in a coffin, or are drawn back again, and their every move is constricted by being subject to royal decree. The aim of Claudius, when his wind is up, is to put Hamlet in 'fetters' (III.3.25). Graveyards, ships and closets are literally confining spaces. More **metaphorically**, the words 'bond', 'bound' and 'bind' are used to convey an obligation of blood and loyalty, an indisputable and unavoidable duty. Hamlet says to the Ghost: 'Speak, I am bound to hear' and receives the reply: 'So art thou to revenge, when thou shalt hear.' The Ghost then tells of his own confinement in the 'prison house' of purgatory (I.5.6–20).

Spying

The Elizabethan secret service is reflected in the play's go-betweens and informers, and in the **imagery** of secrecy and withholding information. This voyeuristic play begins with the watching of the guard and their references to secret preparations. From then on characters are either on watch, watching each other or deliberately spying; there is comprehensive surveillance throughout the play from a battalion of spies. Polonius, Reynaldo, Rosencrantz and Guildenstern, Ophelia and Gertrude — and even Horatio — are asked or offer to report on what they have observed, and Hamlet is 'Th'observed of all observers' (III.1.155). We actually always know more than Hamlet, because we have seen more, and have watched the plots being hatched, but he has a way of seeing which defies mere watching or being present.

He has a 'prophetic soul' which marks him out as an intuitive perceiver, and the audience can merely try to keep up. Much of the play's imagery is concerned with eyes and verbs of seeing, such as 'treason can but peep to what it would' (IV.5.126). The **irony** is that however much watching goes on, being able to interpret accurately what is seen is another matter, and this ability distinguishes the intelligent Claudius from the unintelligent Polonius. Deceit, disguise and betrayal are necessarily involved in the act of spying on someone known to you.

Testing

The concepts of 'probation' and 'proof' are introduced early in the play (I.1.157) and tie in with those of judging, being on trial, and being tempted, which occur in many contexts, for instance in the debate on whether Ophelia should have a Christian burial. Many legal terms are used in the text, and underlying legal issues are touched upon, such as claims to the throne and marriage with one's brother's wife. Hamlet tests the Ghost as well as Claudius with the Mousetrap play; he tests Ophelia and Gertrude when he visits them; he tests providence on several occasions. Testing is fundamental to the plots and morals of biblical and mythological stories, enabling characters (e.g. Adam and Hercules, Judas and Icarus) to rise or fall according to how they respond to temptations and instructions.

Humanity

Kinship and kindness (in the sense of natural behaviour befitting one's species) are introduced in Hamlet's first utterance. He constantly examines and is perplexed by the qualities of humanity, the essence of man and woman, their differences from each other and from animals and how good can become evil. Hamlet finds it hard to reconcile the heroic spirit of man with his ageing flesh and decomposing body. As Ophelia says in a lucid moment, 'We know what we are, but know not what we may be' (IV.5.43–44). To be human is necessarily to be in a state of doubt. By contrast beasts are referred to in I.2.150, I.5.41, II.2.448 and IV.4.35. Hamlet fears being a beast if he either does or does not kill Claudius.

Imagery

Imagery is figurative language, usually **similes** or **metaphors**, which fires the imagination by presenting pictures to the brain. It is a means of making memorable both the everyday and the poignant, and of forcing analogies to be recognised. Imagery can convey **irony** with its double vision, yoking together the actually incongruous but seemingly similar, or vice versa. Shakespeare's imagery repays close study as it is a key to the issues of a work and not just a descriptive aid. Each play has its own peculiar and recurring group of images in addition to the typical and traditional

images of the Elizabethan period, such as those pertaining to heaven and hell, light and dark. The language of the tragedies generally is dominated by life-threatening images of evil, poison, disease and violence.

Image and theme are closely related in Shakespeare's plays, and one is often the concrete version of the other; for example, poison is a metaphor for evil but also the literal cause of death of five characters in the play. Some images are both visual and conceptual; there are real Players in the cast list as well as metaphorical players who are putting on an act; the crossing of two crafts (III.4.211) describes what actually happens on Hamlet's voyage to England. In addition to reinforcing themes, imagery gives atmosphere and progression to a text, helps to delineate character, and provides integrity, pattern and meaning. This play, having an imaginative hero, is particularly based on imaging, and Hamlet's preoccupations are presented in visual terms, such as the Ghost, the skull and the Mousetrap mime.

Earth

The word 'ground' is used as early as I.1.15. Man is a 'quintessence of dust' and clay is the substance from which he was fashioned and in which he is buried; the human cycle is earth to earth. As a place, Hamlet finds it 'stale, flat, and unprofitable' (I.2.133), and weed-ridden. However, the possession of a patch of ground denotes territory, has to be risked all for, and is tied up with identity and honour; Gertrude's body is a metaphorical plot of earth, the possession of it and Denmark being treated as inseparable. Of the four elements, earth is the lowest and heaviest, associated with hell, burial and decay, and the downward movement of the play which attests to the fallen nature of man (e.g. 'throw to earth', I.2.106; 'gross as earth', IV.4.46; 'i'th'cold ground', IV.5.71; 'Though all the earth o'erwhelm them', I.2.258; 'solidity and compound mass', III.4.50). 'Dull', 'dust', 'muddy' and 'grave' are cognate earth words used in many of Hamlet's images. For more than a century, until the Olivier film of 1948, one of the 'points' adopted by actors playing Hamlet was to crawl in either the Mousetrap or the closet scene, stressing his affinity with the earth and actualising his earlier metaphor for all humanity. (The serpent was punished by God in the story of the Fall of Man by losing its legs and being made to crawl henceforth to **symbolise** its low nature.) Hamlet would like to rank among the higher orders of the chain of being, with Hyperion and others who inhabit air and fire, the gods and heroes he refers to so often, to escape his prescribed, earth-bound life in Denmark. The use of the word 'globe', meaning the planet earth, enables **puns** to be made with the human mind and also with the Globe theatre (e.g. I.5.97).

Weeds

Roses are the flowers of choice mentioned in the play several times; they are contrasted with weeds (III.4.152), which represent a quick-spreading and unwholesome product of nature which needs keeping in check because associated in the play (and in the Bible) with evil and corruption. Claudius has polluted the earth by his horrible crime; it is now an 'unweeded garden' (I.2.135). Ophelia drowns in weeds, the envious enemy which strangles and overcomes the flowers with which she is associated. Just as man can be a god or a beast, the earth can produce both the beautiful and the rank.

Burdens

'Load', 'weight', and 'heaviness' are synonyms for 'burden' in the play (e.g. 'Hercules and his load', II.2.360–61). Hercules was depicted as bearing a globe (depicted on the sign for the Globe theatre in which *Hamlet* was performed). Burdens relate to the feeling of melancholy and the image of earth as the heaviest and therefore lowest element. Weighed down by sin, man's soul cannot fly to heaven.

Digging

Adam was sent out of paradise to dig for a living, a point made in the graveyard scene through mention of 'gardeners, ditchers, and grave-makers' (V.1.30). There are references elsewhere to 'moles', 'pioners' and 'enginers' — miners all. Digging holes in the earth, and making graves in particular, links to many of the recurring ideas of the play: imprisonment, hell, man's lowly origin and final resting place, the corruption of the flesh, delving for the truth.

Trapping

'Springes to catch woodcocks' (I.3.115) and 'Your bait of falsehood takes this carp of truth' (II.1.63) are hunting and fishing images. A variety of characters set traps for each other — as Hamlet does with the Mousetrap — and the ironic consequence is that villains are 'hoist with [their] own petar' (III.4.208). Polonius is associated with fishmongery, and Rosencrantz and Guildenstern are also accused of fishing. Hamlet and Claudius vie for the relative roles of fisherman and fish. Hamlet regales him with the image of how a king might progress through the guts of a beggar who ate a fish which had eaten a worm.

Falling

The verb 'fall' is used often in the play (e.g. 'what a falling off was there', I.5.47), evoking the Fall of Man and the relationship of Adam and Eve and Satan, paralleled by old Hamlet, Gertrude and Claudius, who killed his brother in the orchard. Fortune was represented in contemporary art and literature as a heartless female who turns her wheel and causes man's downfall. There are many other references to looking or moving downwards (e.g. 'throw to earth', I.2.106); the first criticism made against Hamlet by Claudius is that he looks down too much, seeking his father

in the dust, and Claudius's words 'fly up' but his thoughts 'remain below' when he is praying. The downward pull of the burdens of guilt and grief are much mentioned, and the prefix 'o'er' appears several times to denote defeat, as in 'o'erthrown' (III.1.151 and III.2.222). The prefix presupposes a concept of hierarchy and the abnormality of things out of place on the chain of being or within understood relations. In addition to Hamlet's mercurial character, with rising and falling mood changes, there is literal falling in the play, as in the various deaths, particularly Ophelia's. Only honour, however finally defined, can redeem man's natural tendencies and raise him up, as Hamlet is raised by Fortinbras at the end of the play and his soul sent heavenwards by the cannon fire.

Eating

Eating is a low activity for humans according to the medieval church, which advocated fasting as often as possible to increase spirituality and the chance of getting to heaven. Old Hamlet is being punished in purgatory for being 'full of bread' and the gateway to hell was represented on medieval and later stages as a gaping mouth. In medieval iconography Death was often depicted as eating his victims and having an insatiable appetite (an idea also used in John Milton's *Paradise Lost*). References to or by Claudius are often accompanied by comments on eating and drinking, giving the impression that he is excessively sensual generally, and guilty of the deadly sins of gluttony and lechery. Hamlet pursues an analogy throughout the play between meat and human flesh, eating and being eaten, which is particularly evident in his comments on Polonius and his 'guts'. He logically connects eating to flesh and flesh to sex, the completion of the syllogism being that eating equals sex (note 'good kissing carrion', II.2.182, where 'carrion' means sexual corruption as well as dead meat).

Poison

This is a complex and frequent image in the play, used to denote internally produced or externally applied evil; a 'dram of evil' can infect the whole body as the corruption spreads. It is used by many characters and appears in the action of the play as well as in its language. In addition to all the literal fatal poisonings in the play (five in all), Ophelia's death is caused by the metaphorical 'poison of deep grief' (IV.5.76), the state in which Hamlet begins the play.

Ears

Ears receive actual poison, or the metaphorical version as slander or unpalatable words. The editors of the Arden edition point out that the play has an 'obsession with literal and metaphorical *ears*' (p. 461); examples occur in I.2.171 and I.3.30. Some commentators argue that Hamlet's ears are infected by the Ghost's poisonous story, which then taints his mind.

Disease

This is a dominant physical and mental image, also occurring as 'eruption', 'canker', 'contagion', 'blastment', 'blister', 'tumour', 'ulcer', and 'ecstasy'. Madness is a 'wit diseased'. A hidden ('filmed') malignity undermines wholesomeness and leads to rottenness, maggots and worms. There is frequent use of the word 'sick', starting on the first page of the text; and Denmark is sick. Whores were branded on the forehead, which caused a blister to warn off men. Old Hamlet's dying body became literally covered with a 'vile and loathsome crust', whereas his widow, according to Hamlet, has metaphorical blisters and ulcers.

Arrows

Arrows appear often, as in 'out of the shot and danger of desire' (I.3.35) and 'That I have shot my arrow o'er the house/And hurt my brother' (V.2.237–38). Hamlet is an arrow shot by Claudius to England which doubles back to Denmark. He learns of this 'sudden and more strange return' immediately after telling Laertes that he could not punish Hamlet as 'my arrows…/Would have reverted to my bow again,/And not where I had aimed them' (IV.7.21–24). The verbs 'shoot' and 'aim' commonly occur to reinforce the theme of outcomes defeating intentions. Daggers, bodkins and rapiers are honorary arrows in the play, and in the case of the latter, also return to kill their owner.

'The imagery enables the basic situation of the play to appear as one in which the beast in man has destroyed the god and now reigns in his kingdom' (Arden edition, p. 438). That man is engaged in an internal battle between animal and angel, higher and lower instincts, is very much a **Renaissance** concept. How man could be made in God's image but fall prey to temptation and bestial appetites, and how evil could have so much destructive power in a divinely created universe, were **paradoxes** which much exercised thinkers from the medieval period onwards. Hence the dilemma for humans, represented by Hamlet, in reading the signs correctly and determining who is in control at any given moment, God or the devil. The play's imagery is negative, as befits a **tragedy**, but man's primeval struggle is to rise, despite all the pitfalls ready to bring him down, and aspire to salvation.

Hamlet's soliloquies

In Shakespeare's plays there is usually empathy between the audience and the characters who speak alone on stage, even such villainous ones as Richard III, and Edmund in *King Lear*. The dramatic device of the **soliloquy** gives us the speaker's perspective and makes us in a way his accomplices, as we are taken into his confidence and listen to his plots being hatched against the other characters. The soliloquy also acts like a chorus, commenting on what has just happened or is about

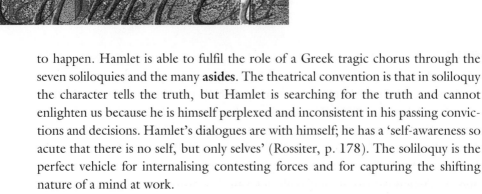

to happen. Hamlet is able to fulfil the role of a Greek tragic chorus through the seven soliloquies and the many **asides**. The theatrical convention is that in soliloquy the character tells the truth, but Hamlet is searching for the truth and cannot enlighten us because he is himself perplexed and inconsistent in his passing convictions and decisions. Hamlet's dialogues are with himself; he has a 'self-awareness so acute that there is no self, but only selves' (Rossiter, p. 178). The soliloquy is the perfect vehicle for internalising contesting forces and for capturing the shifting nature of a mind at work.

One tends to think of Hamlet as being alone and speaking to himself much more often than is in fact the case. For instance, Horatio is definitely present and the Clowns have not been given an 'exeunt' when he muses on Yorick's skull, though this is a visual icon which suggests that Hamlet and the skull are in lone mutual contemplation. However, he is alone for the seven soliloquies, which fosters the idea that he is isolated, needs to be secretive, and has no one he can confide in. Even more than in other plays, the soliloquies are verbalised meditation and seem curiously detachable; indeed, the most famous one appears much earlier (II.2) in Q1 than in the other two texts, and different directors put it in different places. In some productions the actor has addressed the audience directly in his soliloquies. There are things to be both lost and gained by this device. The audience is made to feel uncomfortably involved and implicated in the horrors and moral dilemmas facing Hamlet, which he is sharing with the audience. Theatrical illusion is compromised; but the play also gains because its disconcertingly shifting nature and its multiple levels of audience become further complicated.

The soliloquies take the philosopher's approach of moving out from the particular to the universal, and chart Hamlet's fluctuating emotions, changes of plan and intellectual explorations. The shift from 'I' to 'we' within them shows Hamlet's process of inductive reasoning, drawing general conclusions about mankind from his own particular observations and circumstances, just as he makes damning and sweeping generalisations about womankind from the behaviour of Gertrude and Ophelia. Hamlet always appears to arrive at a conclusion, but it is a purely ephemeral one, and the decision of the moment passes, even when it has been conjured by reasoning rather than by passion. Hamlet has been hailed as the first modern sensibility in literature, in that he has an interiority, a postmodern subjectivity and use of self-reference, a wry acknowledgement of complexity rather than a coherent identity, and a surprisingly modern preoccupation with internally felt guilt, as opposed to shame in the eyes of the external world. The soliloquies have been accused of being a substitute for action, a way of venting impotent rage, as they do not seem to further anything and in fact retard the action; but they define the play and the ironical, introspective, self-critical, conversational essay mode of its intensely self-aware hero.

The soliloquies, and their sequence, convey Hamlet's development as a character as the play progresses. Some end decisively on a couplet at a scene end, the others are interrupted by an entrance. They alternate between deciding to defer action as a result of moral reflection (2,4,6) and reaching a decision to act immediately as a result of adopting a passionate and aggressive position (3,5,7). This inconsistency is entirely in keeping with his ongoing dilemma, and the vacillating double nature of the play and his character, which is that of a manic (bipolar) depressive veering between high and low moods of triumphalism and self-abasement. What the soliloquies all have in common is a quest to turn apprehension into comprehension, and they indicate the stages of his arriving at the resolution of his doubts and willingness to be directed.

Hamlet gives up the soliloquising habit from Act IV scene 4, which gives the impression that he has renounced words, reflection and rational processing, that the time has now come for action, and that events are now moving under a relentless momentum which leaves no time for philosophising or reason to question the powers that be. Hamlet is thereafter distanced from the audience both physically and mentally, as we do not see him alone on stage again and no longer know what he is feeling or planning. Instead, letters take over the plot development instead, Horatio becomes the medium of communication between Hamlet and the audience, and his dialogue with the gravedigger reveals his preoccupation with death and burial.

The seven soliloquies

1   Act I scene 2 lines 129–59

Hamlet is suicidally depressed by his father's death and mother's remarriage. He is disillusioned with life, love and women. Whether 'sullied' (Q2) or 'solid' (F) flesh, the reference is to man's fallen state. This is the fault of woman, because of Eve's sin, and because the misogynistic medieval church had decreed that the father supplied the spirit and the mother the physical element of their offspring. Both words apply equally well, linking with the **theme** of corruption or the **imagery** of heaviness, but 'solid' is more subtle and fits better with the sustained **metaphor** of 'melting', 'dew' and 'moist', and the overarching framework of the four hierarchical elemental levels in the play: fire, air, water and earth. Melancholy was associated with a congealing of the blood, which also supports the 'solid' reading. In all likelihood it is a deliberate **pun** on both words by the dramatist and Hamlet. (A third reading of 'sallied' in Q1, meaning absaulted/assailed, links to the imagery of battle and arrows.)

Other imagery concerns a barren earth, weed-infested and gone to seed, making the soliloquy an **elegy** for a world and father lost. Hamlet condemns his mother for lack of delay, and is concerned about her having fallen 'to incestuous sheets'. His attitude to his dead father, his mother and his new father are all made clear to the audience here, but we may suspect that he has a habit of exaggeration and strong passion, confirmed by his use of three names of mythological characters.

His reference to the sixth commandment — thou shalt not kill — and application of it to suicide as well as murder introduces the first of many Christian precepts in the play and shows Hamlet to be concerned about his spiritual state and the afterlife. Many of the play's images and themes are introduced here, in some cases with their paired opposites: Hyperion versus satyr; heart versus tongue; heaven versus earth; 'things rank and gross in nature'; memory; reason.

2 Act I scene 5 lines 92–112

Having heard the Ghost's testimony, Hamlet becomes distressed and impassioned. He is horrified by the behaviour of Claudius and Gertrude and is convinced he must avenge his father's murder. This speech is duplicative, contains much **tautology**, and is fragmented and confused. To reveal his state of shock he uses **rhetorical** questions, short phrases, dashes and exclamations, and jumps from subject to subject. God is invoked three times. The dichotomy between head and heart is mentioned again.

3 Act II scene 2 lines 546–603

Hamlet's mood shifts from self-loathing to a determination to subdue passion and follow reason, applying this to the testing of the Ghost and his uncle with the play. The first part of the speech mirrors the style of the First Player describing Pyrrhus, with its short phrasing, incomplete lines, melodramatic diction and irregular metre. This is a highly rhetorical speech up to line 585, full of lists, insults and repetitions of vocabulary, especially the word 'villain'; this suggests he is channelling his rage and unpacking his heart with words in this long soliloquy, railing impotently against himself as well as Claudius. He then settles into the gentler and more regular rhythm of thought rather than emotion. The **irony** being conveyed is that cues for passion do not necessarily produce it in reality in the same way that they do in fiction, and that **paradoxically** deep and traumatic feeling can take the form of an apparent lack of, or even inappropriate, manifestation.

4 Act III scene 1 lines 56–89

This was originally the third soliloquy in Q1, and came before the entry of the Players. In Q2 it has been moved to later. Some directors therefore place this most famous of soliloquies at II.2.171, but this has the effect of making Hamlet appear to be meditating on what he has just been reading rather than on life in general whereas the Act III scene 1 placing puts the speech at the centre of the play, where Hamlet has suffered further betrayals and has more reason to entertain suicidal thoughts. The speech uses the general 'we' and 'us', and makes no reference to Hamlet's personal situation or dilemma. Though traditionally played as a soliloquy, technically it is not, as Ophelia appears to be overtly present (and in some productions Hamlet addresses the speech directly to her) and Claudius and Polonius are within earshot. At the time this was a standard 'question' (this being a term used in academic disputation, the way the word 'motion' is now used in debating): whether it is better to live unhappily or not at all. As always, Hamlet moves from the particular to the general, and he asks why humans put up with their burdens and pains when they have a means of escape with a 'bare bodkin'.

Hamlet also questions whether it is better to act or not to act, to be a passive stoic like Horatio or to meet events head on, even if by taking up arms this will lead to one's own death, since they are not to be overcome. There is disagreement by critics (see Rossiter, p. 175) as to whether to 'take up arms against a sea of troubles' ends one's opponent or oneself, but it would seem to mean the latter in the context. Though humans can choose whether to die or not, they have no control over 'what dreams may come', and this thought deters him from embracing death at this stage. Though death is 'devoutly to be wished' because of its promise of peace, it is to be feared because of its mystery, and reason will always counsel us to stick with what we know. Strangely, the Ghost does not seem to count in Hamlet's mind as a 'traveller' who 'returns'. Given that Hamlet has already concluded that he cannot commit suicide because 'the Everlasting had...fixed/His canon 'gainst self-slaughter', there is no reason to think he has changed his mind about such a fundamental moral and philosophical imperative.

C. S. Lewis (Lerner, p. 72) claims that Hamlet does not suffer from a fear of dying, but from a fear of being dead, of the unknown and unknowable. However, Hamlet later comes to see that this is a false dichotomy, since one can collude with fate rather than try futilely to resist it, and then have nothing to fear. The 'conscience' which makes us all cowards probably means conscience in the modern sense, as it does in 'catch the conscience of the King' (II.2.603). However, its other meaning of 'thought' is equally appropriate, and the double meaning encapsulates the human condition: to be capable of reason means inevitably to recognise one's guilt, and both thought and guilt make us fear punishment in the next life. With the exception of Claudius, intermittently and not overridingly, and Gertrude after being schooled by Hamlet, no other character in the play shows evidence of having a conscience in the sense of being able to judge oneself and be self-critical.

This has a slower pace than the previous soliloquies, a higher frequency of adjectives, metaphors, rhythmical repetitions, and regular **iambics**. Hamlet's melancholy and doubt show through in the use of **hendiadys**, the stress on disease, burdens, pain and weapons, and the generally jaundiced world view. The 'rub' referred to in line 65 is an allusion to an obstacle in a game of bowls which deflects the bowl from its intended path, and is yet another indirection metaphor.

5 Act III scene 2 lines 395–406

Now Hamlet feels ready to proceed against the guilty Claudius. He is using the stereotypical avenger language and tone in what the Arden edition calls 'the traditional night-piece apt to prelude a deed of blood' (p. 511). He is aping the previous speaker's mode as so often, trying to motivate himself to become a stage villain, by identifying with Lucianus, the nephew to the king. This is the least convincing of his soliloquies because of the crudity of the clichéd utterance, and one suspects it is a leftover from an earlier version of the revenge play. The emphasis at the end, however, is on avoiding violence and showing concern for his own and his mother's souls; his great fear is of being 'unnatural', behaving as a monster like Claudius. He is, however, impressionable to theatrical performance, as we saw from his reaction to the Pyrrhus/Hecuba speeches earlier, and this carries him through to the slaying of Polonius before it wears off and, if we can believe it, ''A weeps for what is done'. This soliloquy creates tension for the audience, who are unsure of how his first private meeting with his mother will turn out and how they will speak to each other. He mentions his 'heart' and 'soul' again.

6   Act III scene 3 lines 73–96

Hamlet decides not to kill Claudius while he is praying, claiming that this would send him to heaven, which would not be a fitting punishment for a man who killed his father unprepared for death and sent him to purgatory. For Hamlet revenge must involve justice. It begins with a hypothetical 'might', as if he has already decided to take no action, confirmed by the single categorical word 'No' in line 87, the most decisive utterance in the play. The usual diction is present: 'heaven' (4), 'hell', 'black', 'villain' (2), 'sickly', 'soul' (2), 'heavy', 'thought', 'act'.

7   Act IV scene 4 lines 32–66

Hamlet questions why he has delayed, and the nature of man and honour. He resolves again to do the bloody deed. Once again, he is not really alone; he has told Rosencrantz and Guildenstern to move away but they are still on stage, following their orders to watch him.

Despite exhortation and exclamation at the end, this speech excites Hamlet's blood for no longer than the previous soliloquies. Though it seems to deprecate passive forbearance and endorse the nobility of action — by definition one cannot be great if one merely refrains — the negative diction of 'puffed', 'eggshell', 'straw', 'fantasy' and 'trick' work against the meaning so that it seems ridiculous of Fortinbras to be losing so much to gain so little, and neither Hamlet nor the audience can be persuaded of the alleged honour to be gained. Fortinbras — who is not really a 'delicate and tender prince' but a ruthless and militaristic one, leader of a 'list of lawless resolutes' (I.1.98) — seems positively irresponsible in his willingness to sacrifice 20,000 men for a tiny patch of ground and a personal reputation. Critics dispute whether Hamlet is condemning himself and admiring Fortinbras, having accepted that the way to achieve greatness is to fight and win, like his father, or whether he has now realised how ridiculous the quest for honour is, and that one should wait for it to come rather than seek it out. As the Arden editors point out, there is double-think going on, whereby 'Hamlet insists on admiring Fortinbras while at the same time acknowledging the absurdity of his actions' (p. 371). As so often when Hamlet is debating with himself and playing his own devil's advocate, the opposite meaning seems to defeat the conscious argument he is trying to present. Lines 53 to 56 are grammatically obscure and add to the confusion. What is clear is Hamlet's frustration with himself at the beginning of the soliloquy, which the 26 monosyllables comprising lines 43–46 powerfully convey.

Quotations

The best quotations to know are those which you have found useful in class discussions and practice essays, and they will require little conscious learning because you are already familiar with them. The most effective ones to learn in addition are those which serve more than one purpose, i.e. which can be used to support a reference to a theme or image as well as make a point about character or dramatic effect. Think about which points each quotation below could be used to support in an examination or coursework essay.

Act I scene 1

This bodes some strange eruption to our state. (*l. 69, Horatio to Marcellus about the Ghost*)

Act I scene 2

A little more than kin, and less than kind! (*l. 65, Hamlet's aside about Claudius*)

'Seems', madam? Nay, it is. I know not 'seems'. (*l. 76, Hamlet to Gertrude*)

For they are actions that a man might play./But I have that within which passes show —/These but the trappings and the suits of woe. (*ll. 84–86, Hamlet to Gertrude about grief*)

We pray you throw to earth/This unprevailing woe, and think of us/As of a father. (*ll. 106–08, Claudius to Hamlet*)

How weary, stale, flat, and unprofitable/Seem to me all the uses of this world! (*ll. 133–34, Hamlet about life*)

Frailty, thy name is woman. (*l. 146, Hamlet about Gertrude*)

The funeral baked meats/Did coldly furnish forth the marriage tables. (*ll. 180–01, Hamlet to Horatio about his mother's wedding*)

'A was a man. Take him for all in all,/I shall not look upon his like again. (*ll. 187–88, Hamlet to Horatio about his father*)

Foul deeds will rise,/Though all the earth o'erwhelm them, to men's eyes. (*ll. 257–58, Hamlet alone*)

Act I scene 3

His greatness weighed, his will is not his own. (*l. 17, Laertes to Ophelia about Hamlet*)

Act I scene 4

So horridly to shake our disposition/With thoughts beyond the reaches of our souls?/Say, why is this? Wherefore? What should we do? (*ll. 55–57, Hamlet to Ghost*)

I do not set my life at a pin's fee. (*l. 65, Hamlet to Horatio*)

My fate cries out… (*l. 81, Hamlet to Horatio*)

Something is rotten in the state of Denmark. (*l. 90, Marcellus to Horatio*)

Act I scene 5

The serpent that did sting thy father's life/Now wears his crown. (*ll. 39–40, Ghost to Hamlet about Claudius*)

No reckoning made, but sent to my account/With all my imperfections on my head. (*ll. 78–9, Ghost to Hamlet about his murder*)

If thou hast nature in thee, bear it not. (*l. 81, Ghost to Hamlet about revenge*)

That one may smile, and smile, and be a villain. (*l. 108, Hamlet about Claudius*)

These are but wild and whirling words, my lord. (*l. 133, Horatio to Hamlet*)

There are more things in heaven and earth, Horatio,/Than are dreamt of in your philosophy. (*ll. 166–67, Hamlet about Ghost*)

To put an antic disposition on… (*l. 172, Hamlet to Horatio and Marcellus*)

The time is out of joint. O, cursèd spite,/That ever I was born to set it right! (*ll. 188–89, Hamlet to Horatio*)

Act II scene 1

With windlasses and with assays of bias,/By indirections find directions out. (*ll. 65–66, Polonius to Reynaldo*)

Act II scene 2

Doubt truth to be a liar./But never doubt I love. (*ll. 117–18, Hamlet in love letter to Ophelia*)

Denmark's a prison. (*l. 243, Hamlet to Rosencrantz and Guildenstern*)

For there is nothing either good or bad but thinking makes it so. (*ll. 248–49, Hamlet to Rosencrantz and Guildenstern*)

What a piece of work is a man, how noble in reason...in apprehension how like a god...And yet to me what is this quintessence of dust? (*ll. 303–08, Hamlet to Rosencrantz and Guildenstern*)

And like a neutral to his will and matter/Did nothing. (*ll. 479–80, First Player describing Pyrrhus*)

Use every man after his desert, and who shall 'scape whipping? (*ll. 527–28, Hamlet to Polonius*)

The play's the thing/Wherein I'll catch the conscience of the King. (*ll. 602–03, Hamlet*)

Act III scene 1

'Tis too much proved, that with devotion's visage/And pious action we do sugar o'er/The devil himself. (*ll. 47–49, Polonius to Ophelia*)

Thus conscience does make cowards of us all;/And thus the native hue of resolution/Is sicklied o'er with the pale cast of thought,/And enterprises of great pitch and moment/With this regard their currents turn awry/And lose the name of action. (*ll. 83–88, Hamlet*)

Get thee to a nunnery. Why wouldst thou be a breeder of sinners? (*ll. 121–22, Hamlet to Ophelia*)

What should such fellows as I do crawling between earth and heaven? (*ll. 127–28, Hamlet to Ophelia*)

O, what a noble mind is here o'erthrown!/The courtier's, soldier's, scholar's, eye, tongue, sword,/Th'expectancy and rose of the fair state,/The glass of fashion and the mould of form,/Th'observed of all observers, quite, quite, down! (*ll. 151–55, Ophelia about Hamlet*)

There's something in his soul/O'er which his melancholy sits on brood... (*ll. 165–66, Claudius to Polonius about Hamlet*)

Madness in great ones must not unwatched go. (*l. 189, Claudius to Polonius about Hamlet*)

Act III scene 2

Suit the action to the word, the word to the action (*ll. 17–18, Hamlet to First Player*)

And blest are those/Whose blood and judgement are so well commeddled/That they are not a pipe for Fortune's finger/To sound what stop she please. (*ll.78–81, Hamlet to Horatio about Horatio*)

A second time I kill my husband dead/When second husband kisses me in bed. (*ll.194–95, Player Queen to Player King*)

Purpose is but the slave to memory,/Of violent birth, but poor validity... (*ll. 198–99, Player King to Player Queen*)

Our wills and fates do so contrary run/That our devices still are overthrown./Our thoughts are ours, their ends none of our own. (*ll. 221–23, Player King to Player Queen*)

Act III scene 4

Thou wretched, rash, intruding fool, farewell!/I took thee for thy better. Take thy fortune. (*ll. 32–33, Hamlet to dead Polonius*)

A king of shreds and patches… (*l. 103, Hamlet to Gertrude about Claudius*)

It will but skin and film the ulcerous place/Whiles rank corruption, mining all within,/Infects unseen. (*ll. 148–50, Hamlet to Gertrude about her believing him mad*)

But heaven hath pleased it so,/To punish me with this, and this with me,/That I must be their scourge and minister. (*ll. 174–76, Hamlet to Gertrude*)

For 'tis the sport to have the enginer/Hoist with his own petar; (*ll. 207–08, Hamlet to Gertrude about Rosencrantz and Guildenstern*)

Act IV scene 3

Diseases desperate grown/By desperate appliance are relieved… (*ll. 9–10, Claudius to attendants about Hamlet's behaviour*)

Act IV scene 4

What is a man,/If his chief good and market of his time/Be but to sleep and feed? (*ll. 33–35, Hamlet*)

I do not know/Why yet I live to say 'This thing's to do',/Sith I have cause, and will, and strength, and means/To do't. (*ll. 43–46, Hamlet*)

O, from this time forth,/My thoughts be bloody, or be nothing worth! (*ll. 65–66, Hamlet*)

Act IV scene 5

Lord, we know what we are, but know not what we may be. (*ll. 43–44, Ophelia to Claudius*)

Act IV scene 7

…my arrows,/Too slightly timbered for so loud a wind,/Would have reverted to my bow again,/And not where I had aimed them. (*ll. 21–24, Claudius to Laertes about punishing Hamlet*)

He, being remiss,/Most generous, and free from all contriving… (*ll. 133–34, Claudius to Laertes about Hamlet*)

Act V scene 1

'Twere to consider too curiously to consider so. (*l. 202, Horatio to Hamlet about death*)

I loved you ever. But it is no matter./Let Hercules himself do what he may,/The cat will mew, and dog will have his day. (*ll. 286–88, Hamlet to Laertes*)

Act V scene 2

There's a divinity that shapes our ends,/Rough-hew them how we will… (*ll. 10–11, Hamlet to Horatio*)

Being thus be-netted round with villainies,/Or I could make a prologue to my brains/They had begun the play. (*ll. 29–31, Hamlet to Horatio about finding Claudius's letter*)

Why, even in that was heaven ordinant. (*l. 48, Hamlet to Horatio about father's signet ring*)

'Tis dangerous when the baser nature comes/Between the pass and fell incensèd points/Of mighty opposites. (*ll. 60–62, Hamlet to Horatio about death of Rosencrantz and Guildenstern*)

And is't not to be damned/To let this canker of our nature come/In further evil? (*ll. 68–70, Hamlet to Horatio about Claudius*)

But thou wouldst not think how ill all's here about my heart. But it is no matter. (*ll. 206–07, Hamlet to Horatio about duel*)

There is special providence in the fall of a sparrow. …The readiness is all. …Let be. (*ll. 213–18, Hamlet to Horatio*)

…as a woodcock to mine own springe…/I am justly killed with mine own treachery. (*ll. 300–01, Laertes to Osrick*)

…the rest is silence. (*l. 352, Hamlet's last words*)

So shall you hear/Of carnal, bloody, and unnatural acts,/Of accidental judge-ments, casual slaughters/…And, in this upshot, purposes mistook/Fallen on th'inventors' heads. (*ll. 374–79, Horatio to Fortinbras and English ambassadors*)

Let four captains/Bear Hamlet like a soldier to the stage./For he was likely, had he put on,/To have proved most royal. (*ll. 389–92, Fortinbras*)

Critical comments

The following comments by critics show changing attitudes over four centuries towards the play or its main character. They could be useful to support your own opinion in a coursework or exam essay or to provide evidence of alternative views.

We must allow to the tragedy of Hamlet the praise of variety. (As below)

Hamlet is, through the whole play, rather an instrument than an agent. (Samuel Johnson, *Preface to Shakespeare*, 1765)

He is the most amiable of misanthropes. (William Hazlitt, *Characters of Shakespeare's Plays*, 1817)

Hamlet is brave and careless of death; but he vacillates from sensibility, and procrastinates from thought, and loses the power of action in the energy of resolve. (As below)

[Hamlet has] an overbalance of the contemplative faculty…in resolving to do everything, he does nothing. (Samuel Taylor Coleridge, *Lectures and Notes on Shakespeare*, 1818)

The whole story turns upon the peculiar character of the hero. (A. C. Bradley, *Shakespearean Tragedy*, 1904)

Was ever a tragic figure so torn and tortured! (Ernest Jones, *Hamlet and Oedipus*, 1910)

I had always felt an aversion from Hamlet: a creeping, unclean thing he seems, on stage…his nasty poking and sniffing at his mother, his setting traps for the king, his conceited perversion with Ophelia make him always intolerable. The character is repulsive in its conception, based on a self-dislike and a spirit of disintegration. (D. H. Lawrence, *Twilight in Italy*, 1913)

Hamlet was not a single consistent character: like most men he was half a dozen characters rolled into one. (George Bernard Shaw, *Letter to Alfred Cruickshank*, 1918)

More people have thought *Hamlet* a work of art because they found it interesting, than have found it interesting because it is a work of art. (As below)

The play is most certainly an artistic failure. (T. S. Eliot, 'Hamlet and his problems', 1922)

The story of a 'sweet prince' wrenched from life and dedicate alone to death. (As below)

Hamlet denies the existence of romantic values.

Hamlet is an element of evil in the state of Denmark.

Hamlet's soul is sick. The symptoms are horror at the fact of death and an equal detestation of life. (G. Wilson Knight, *The Wheel of Fire*, 1930)

The difficulty, in ultimate terms, is to know what the play is really about. (A. J. A. Waldock, *Hamlet: A Study in Critical Method*, 1931)

Hamlet is dominated by an emotion which is inexpressible, because it is in *excess* of the facts as they appear. (T. S. Eliot, *Selected Essays*, 1932)

I would not cross the room to meet Hamlet. It would never be necessary. He is always where I am. (As below)

[Hamlet is] a dishevelled man whose words make us at once think of loneliness and doubt and dread, of waste and dust and emptiness, and from whose hands, or from our own, we feel the richness of heaven and earth and the comfort of human affection slipping away. (C. S. Lewis, *Hamlet: The Prince or the Poem*, 1942)

Hamlet is the most problematic play ever written by Shakespeare or any other playwright. (Harry Levin, *Shakespeare Quarterly*, 1956)

[Hamlet is] the conscience-stricken but paralyzed liberal. (Charles Marowitz, *Hamlet Collage*, 1965)

Hamlet is first to last a creature of circumstance: neither good nor bad, because direction by pure eventuality excludes responsibility and leaves only a conditioned machine, a tortured automaton. (Kenneth Muir, *Shakespeare's 'Hamlet'*, 1987)

Hamlet is…so much too good for his fate. That is the central conflict of the play: the clash between what we feel for the intelligence, generosity, fineness of Hamlet, and the fortuitousness, meanness and clumsiness of the forces by which he is destroyed. (As below)

[Hamlet is] the type of 'modern' or post-Renaissance man: a man essentially divided within and against himself, and…necessarily at war with circumstance. (A. P. Rossiter, *Angel with Horns: 15 Lectures on Shakespeare*, 1989)

…the whole idea of dramatic character is changed for ever by this play…no one much like Hamlet ever existed before. …The new mastery is a mastery of the ambiguous, the unexpected, of conflicting evidence and semantic audacity. (Frank Kermode, *Shakespeare's Language*, 2000)

Literary terms and concepts

The terms and concepts below have been selected for their relevance to talking and writing about *Hamlet*. It will aid argument and expression to become familiar with them and to use them in your essays, provided you can support them with examples from the text and explain their effect.

Literary terms

ambiguity	capacity of words to have two simultaneous meanings in the same context, either accidentally or, more often, as a deliberate device for enriching the meaning of text, e.g. 'questionable shape'
anagnorisis	moment of recognition by a character of an important truth
antithesis	contrast of ideas expressed by balancing words or phrases of opposite meaning, e.g. being cruel to be kind
archetype	original model used as a recurrent symbol, e.g. the brave warrior
aside	remark spoken by a character in a play which is shared with the audience but unheard by some or all of the other characters on stage
blank verse	unrhymed **iambic pentameter**, the staple form of Shakespeare's plays

caesura	deliberate break or pause in a line of poetry, signified by punctuation
circumlocutio	'talking around' a subject rather than referring to it directly, used for comic effect or to build tension, e.g. I.1.35–39
climax	moment of intensity to which a series of actions has been leading
colloquial	in the informal language of speech rather than the more formal language of writing
crux (plural **cruces**)	point of critical argument or controversy in a text, e.g. 'sullied' versus 'solid'
dénouement	unfolding of the final stages of a plot, when all is revealed
double entendre	phrase with two meanings, one of them indecent
dramatic irony	when the audience knows something the character speaking does not, which creates tension and is an element of tragedy
elegy	lament for the death or permanent loss of someone or something, e.g. Gertrude's account of Ophelia's drowning
enjambement	run-on instead of end-stopped line of poetry
eulogy	a speech in undiluted (possibly excessive) praise of somebody or something
genre	type or form of writing
hendiadys	figure of speech in which two nouns or adjectives joined by 'and' modify or repeat a single idea, e.g. 'My soul is full of discord and dismay'
hyperbole	deliberate exaggeration for effect, e.g. Hamlet calling his father Hyperion
iambic pentameter	five **feet** of iambs, i.e. alternating unstressed and stressed syllables, the staple metre of Shakespeare's plays
idiolect	style of speech peculiar to an individual character
imagery	figurative descriptive language; a pattern of related images that helps to build up mood and atmosphere and develop the themes of a literary work
in medias res	literally 'in the middle of things', this term applies to speeches begun before the audience joins them, as in the opening of Act III scene 1
interlocutor	the person to whom a character is speaking
irony	discrepancy between the actual and implied meaning of language; or an amusing or cruel reversal of an outcome expected, intended or deserved; situation in which one is mocked by fate or the facts

metafiction	fictional construct which self-consciously and ironically exposes the devices of fiction
metaphor	suppressed comparison, implied not stated, e.g. 'A serpent stung me'
oxymoron	phrase consisting of a contradiction in terms, e.g. 'paragon of animals'
paradox	self-contradictory but true statement or state of affairs, e.g. being cruel to be kind
pathos	pity evoked by a situation of suffering and helplessness
poetic justice	due allocation of reward and punishment for virtue and vice respectively
pun	use of a word with double meaning for humorous or ironic effect, e.g. 'matter' in Act II scene 2
rhetoric	art of persuasion, using emotive language and **syntactical** devices
rhyming couplet	pair of adjacent rhyming lines
Romance	story of love and heroism, deriving from medieval court life and fairy tale
sententia	opinion, maxim; received wisdom
simile	comparison introduced by 'as' or 'like'; an **epic simile** is a lengthy and detailed analogy
soliloquy	speech by character alone on stage which reveals their thoughts
sources	stories or inspirations, drawn from history, mythology or other literary works, which writers build into their own artistic creations
stichomythia	a dramatic technique whereby a series of short speeches are given to alternating speakers in a battle of wits, e.g. in the closet scene
symbol	object, person or event which represents something more than itself, e.g. flowers for Ophelia
tautology	repeating the same idea in different words (e.g. 'melt, thaw, resolve itself into a dew') to delay the delivery of the sentiment or for pretentious or poetic effect
theme	idea or issue explored in a literary work, as distinct from the content
tragedy	drama or other literary work of a serious nature traditionally concerning men in high positions, with a fatal conclusion for both the guilty and the innocent; characterised by waste, loss and a fall from power.
verse	language organised according to its rhythmical qualities into regular patterns of metre and set out in lines

Literary concepts

Cain and Abel	story in Genesis of the first sons of Adam and Eve; Cain committed the first murder by killing his brother Abel
catharsis	Aristotle claimed that **tragedy** achieves catharsis (Greek for purging) for the audience because of the feelings of pity and fear which it evokes
divine idiot	stereotype of someone, often an epileptic, considered foolish but nearer to God for being simple and uncorrupted; also called **holy fool**
dualism	philosophical system that recognises two fundamental principles in the scheme of things, such as mind and matter, or good and evil
eternal verity	universal wisdom allegedly shared by all civilised cultures
Everyman	title of a fifteenth-century morality play, it has come to stand for an ordinary individual confronted by a choice between good and evil, and summoned by Death
fin de siècle	French for 'end of the century' (and first used about the year 1900), it expresses the social angst and insecurity which writers express in works spanning a turn of a century and end of an era because society is facing an unknown future
golden mean	the felicitous middle between two extremes, one of excess and one of deficiency, viewed by Aristotle, an ancient Greek philospher, as the finest guiding principle of human conduct
gothic	artistic and literary genre inspired by the medieval period, containing violence, death, horror, the supernatural and the macabre; set in eerie ancient locations, such as castles and graveyards, often during darkness and cold or bad weather
hubris	exaggerated self-pride or self-confidence, taking the form of a human getting above himself, resulting in a fall as the fatal retribution administered by the goddess Nemesis
Machiavellian	describing early sixteenth-century political philosophy proposed by the Italian Niccolo Machiavelli in his book *The Prince*, which recommended ruthless self-interest and unethical methods to gain political power
memento mori	Latin for 'Remember your death'; an artistic symbol of mortality, typically a flower, a skull or an hourglass

microcosm/ macrocosm	states and occurrences in the individual organism, e.g. violence or conflict, are magnified and reflected in larger contexts, e.g. war, tempest. The state of Denmark reflects the problems in the royal family.
noblesse oblige	belief that noble birth imposes the obligation of high-minded principles and honorable actions
objective correlative	term popularised by T. S. Eliot in his essay 'Hamlet and His Problems', when explaining his view that the chain of events as given did not justify Hamlet's extreme emotional reaction to them; an appropriate matching of emotion to object
Oedipus complex	Freud's term for the psychological state of a male who subconsciously wishes to kill his father and marry his mother, and the double guilt arising from these prohibited desires. In the Greek myth, Oedipus blinded himself and went into exile after discovering that he had murdered his father and married his own mother.
philistine	uncultured biblical race (the Philistines); someone who despises art, beauty, intellectual and spiritual values
psychomachia	literally 'battle of the mind', this term was used to describe an internal mental struggle between good and evil
Renaissance	originating in Italy, the revival of art and literature under the influence of classical models in the fifteenth and sixteenth centuries in Western Europe
Romantic	artistic period of late eighteenth and early nineteenth centuries, characterised by a rebellious assertion of belief in the spiritual correspondence between man and nature, and a recognition of the necessity of passion as a counterbalance to reason
Seneca	an optimistic humanist in his essays, Seneca is more commonly associated with bloody revenge tragedy
seven deadly sins	according to the medieval Catholic church, the following sins were mortal and led straight to hell: pride, envy, gluttony, lechery, avarice, wrath, sloth; many contemporary and later literary works include these sins symbolically or thematically
Stoic	follower of ancient Greek moral doctrine that happiness consists in liberation from passions and appetites, and therefore from suffering

Trojan War	basis of Homer's *Iliad*, which tells the tale of Helen's abduction by the Trojan Prince Paris and the ten-year siege of Troy by the Greeks (including her husband King Menelaus and Odysseus, King of Ithaca) to get her back; the literary paradigm for all love and war stories, concerning honour, revenge, betrayal, deceit (the Trojan horse), military prowess, a doomed royal family, and the fall of an empire
Zeitgeist	German for 'spirit of the time', the outlook characteristic of a particular age

Questions & Answers

Essay questions, specimen plans and notes

Coursework essays

Below are some titles which would be appropriate for a coursework essay.

1 **Explore how Shakespeare examines the themes of loyalty and betrayal in *Hamlet*. Compare your interpretation of *Hamlet* with those of other critics.**

You should refer to the following:

- the characteristics of Shakespearean tragedy
- the key scenes which address the themes of loyalty and betrayal
- the dramatic impact these scenes would have on the audience
- how the original audience would have responded differently from a modern one
- how issues linked to loyalty and betrayal are revealed to the audience through characters, imagery and language
- how Hamlet contributes to the portrayal of these themes
- how themes of loyalty and betrayal have been commented on by various critics
- Hamlet as the tragic hero
- Hamlet's treatment of other characters
- Hamlet compared to other characters
- how Hamlet has been viewed by various critics
- your own view on how the themes of loyalty and betrayal are shown and developed in the play
- your own interpretation of *Hamlet*

Further questions

2 **What interests you most about the play of *Hamlet*? Give a detailed analysis of the complexities and challenges of the play as far as a modern audience is concerned.**

3 **What are Hamlet the character and *Hamlet* the play saying about the concept of evil, and how do these views relate to those of the society the play was written in?**

4 **Explore the character of Hamlet, showing how he develops through the play and comparing your views with those of other commentators.**

5 **Do you consider *Hamlet* to be primarily a political or a domestic drama? Consider both interpretations of the play, and explain how the two dimensions relate to each other.**

6 **Compare Hamlet to two other characters in the play for similarity and contrast; choose from Claudius, Polonius, Fortinbras, Horatio and Laertes.**

7 **How does Shakespeare portray women in the play? Examine the characterisation and function of the female characters.**

8 Write about the use of imagery in *Hamlet* and its contribution to the overall effect of the play.

9 What have you gained in your knowledge of Shakespeare and his period by your study of *Hamlet*?

10 Examine the various conflicts and tensions of a changing society presented in *Hamlet*, and explain their significance for the main character.

11 What are the major points of disagreement between the critics about this play? Where do your own judgements and sympathies lie?

12 Which concerns of the play alienate modern readers, and which can they more readily empathise with?

Exam essays

The exemplar essay questions that follow can be used for planning practice and/or full essay writing within the time limit, with or without the text. Many have been previously set by different exam boards for various specifications. In each of the following sections there are some essay titles with suggestions for ideas to include in a plan, and some with examiners' notes and guidance on how to approach the question. Two questions are provided with sample student answers.

Remember to talk about the play and the audience, not the book and the reader, and try to visualise how it would look on stage and imagine how it would sound; the drama and the poetry are essential elements of the written text you are being asked to respond to. Here are the questions to address when analysing drama text passages:

- Is it all verse, all prose, or a mixture?
- Is it primarily looking forward to something which is to come, or looking backwards to explain or reinforce a previous event? The right answer will usually be both; the graveyard scene, for example, conveys Hamlet's isolation and pre-occupation with the afterlife as well as preparing for the duel between himself and Laertes, and his own death.
- Are there any entrances or exits, and what effect do they have if so?
- Look at stage directions. What are the visual effects of the position of props and the actions being performed?
- Identify themes and make links to their appearance elsewhere in the play.
- Comment on the imagery, relate it to similar or contrasting usages, and explain its link with themes.
- Is there a dominant or silent presence or one who is given relatively few lines? How might the positions or grouping of the characters suggest support for or opposition to each other?
- Is there any irony or dramatic irony? Who knows what at this stage?
- With whom is the audience's sympathy, and why?
- How does this passage relate to others elsewhere? Is it similar or a contrast to another episode?

Hamlet **111**

- How does the language and its tone reveal character, and how does it affect the audience's feelings about something or someone?
- How does the scene add to plot and character, themes and language? Why does it exist, and why at this point?

Whole-text questions: open text

Note: some of the questions in this section could be suitable as closed-text questions.

1 'It is essential to the development of the play's tragic situation that Hamlet, Laertes and Fortinbras are trained fighters.' How far do you agree with this view? In your answer you should discuss characters and motives, narrative development and setting. You should also show an awareness of Elizabethan attitudes to gender and honour, as well as an awareness of Shakespearean tragedy.

Top band descriptors:

AO1 Lucid expression in a relevant and well-organised answer.

AO3 Perceptive and detailed insight into the varying soldier characters of the play, their military status and accompanying attitudes – to honour, to women, to reputation, for example; and sensitivity to Shakespeare's handling of the military setting and development of the narrative arising from the motivation of the soldiers in defence of their honour.

AO4 Mature and thoughtful judgement of the critical view expressed, weighing how far it can be accepted and why – the word 'essential' may be challenged; informed by an awareness of differing points of view.

AO5i Good understanding of Elizabethan attitudes to territory acquisition, military and personal honour and the structure of Shakespearean tragedy.

2 Montaigne said about life: 'All is but changing, motion, and inconstancy.' Explore the nature and significance of the continuous mental and physical shifting in *Hamlet*. Explain how it links to the overall themes of the play.

Possible ideas for a plan:

- the Penguin introduction describes play as having 'inconsistencies, discontinuities and mercurial shifts', which are related symptoms of breakdown of order
- political background of an aged monarch without heir and uncertainty for the future of England
- Denmark has four kings in the framework of the play: old Hamlet, Claudius, Hamlet, Fortinbras
- innovation not well viewed at that time; Hamlet makes his dislike of the new and preference for the old clear on several occasions, e.g. theatre companies
- it is the sudden shift in his family structure which has plunged Hamlet into a state of melancholy
- tradition and custom were important to social stability and the safeguarding of values
- the play constantly shifts physical ground and the scenes are in a variety of venues

- the action involves much travelling by many characters: Fortinbras, ambassadors, Rosencrantz and Guildenstern, Laertes, Players
- Hamlet physically journeys but is also on a spiritual journey 'into the abyss of himself' (Yeats) and towards the end of the road of life
- the imagery refers constantly to heaven, earth and hell, the different cosmic levels, and man's movement between them
- the imagery also relies on action verbs of falling, digging, shooting, crossing
- Hamlet's passions fluctuate and his moods and decisions change manically, e.g. after the success of the Mousetrap; the difference between soliloquies 2 and 3, and 4 and 5
- the constant interruptions and entrances and exits cause lack of continuity and quick changes of topic
- the madness of Hamlet and Ophelia add further bewildering shifts of personality; Gertrude also changes in the play, as does Horatio at the end
- there are 11 deaths enacted or referred to (including old Fortinbras and Yorick) which is a lot even for a Shakespeare tragedy; a death is an absolute and sudden shift of status to corpse, e.g. Polonius
- the appearance of the Ghost shifts Hamlet's moral universe, divorcing his present from his past and denying him a future; nothing can ever be the same again for him
- the instability and unpredictability of human existence form the basis of the themes of doubt and insecurity, fickleness and memory
- Hamlet wants to believe in absolutes and constants, eternal verities, unchanging ways of recognising good and evil, but this is not possible in a world in which everything is relative (nothing good or ill but thinking makes it so), accidental and coincidental

Further questions

3 'Hamlet's delay is absurd.' Discuss the validity of this dismissive view of *Hamlet*.

4   There are more things in heaven and earth, Horatio
        Than are dreamt of in your philosophy.
What do you think Hamlet is referring to, and how is this comment relevant to the play as a whole?

5 Discuss Shakespeare's portrayal of madness in *Hamlet*.

6   Adieu, adieu, adieu. Remember me.

        Purpose is but the slave to memory,
        Of violent birth, but poor validity.
Discuss the role of memory in *Hamlet*.

7 'Deception in the play is not confined to Claudius.' Where else is it important?

8 Hamlet says 'Frailty! Thy name is woman.' How far do you think this applies to Gertrude and Ophelia?

9 C. S. Lewis said that *Hamlet* 'is a mysterious play in the sense of being a play about mystery'. What have you found mysterious about the play?

10 'Hamlet's soul is sick. The symptoms are horror at the fact of death and an equal detestation of life.' What is the evidence to support Wilson Knight's interpretation of the central character?

11 'The enduring interest of the play is its treatment of doubt and indecision.' Do you agree?

12 'This is the story of a man who is visited and destroyed by a ghost.' Do you believe that this is a fair summary of *Hamlet*?

13 '*Hamlet* is the tragedy of a man who couldn't make up his mind.' Is this a satisfactory description of the play?

14 'Hamlet is, through the whole play, rather an instrument than an agent' (Dr Johnson). What do you think is the difference between an 'instrument' and an 'agent', and which do you think Hamlet is?

15 'From the moment the ghost appears to Hamlet in Act I scene 4 he is a marked man on the road to death.' Explain how the play makes this clear.

16 How do Hamlet's first words 'A little more than kin, and less than kind' prefigure his character and preoccupations, and how do they connect to the themes of the play as a whole?

17 'The crowning irony of *Hamlet* is that Hamlet finally achieves his object by accident.' Is this true? Discuss this claim with general reference to irony and accident in the play.

18 'Hamlet...is by no means an ideal figure. Like many avengers, he becomes the deed's creature.' Is this how you feel about Hamlet?

19 What is the importance of the Players and their play to *Hamlet* as a whole?

Whole-text questions: closed text

Note: some of the questions in this section could be suitable as open-text questions.

1 'Something is rotten in the state of Denmark.' Explore the idea of rottenness in *Hamlet*, and explain the significance of this quotation to the play as a whole.

Possible ideas for a plan:

- word 'rotten' used many times, and part of a semantic cluster with 'black', 'unwholesome', 'rank', etc.
- ghosts, war, disorder/lack of harmony all early indications of the state being 'out of joint'
- Ophelia asks what has happened to 'the beauteous majesty of Denmark'
- link to earth where things rot, especially dead flesh
- link to poison, which causes corruption and contagion
- link to madness, which is a 'wit diseased'
- link to sexuality (especially incest and adultery), which breeds sin and is indulgence in appetite, related to Fall and serpent

- tricks, spying, dissimulation all kinds of rottenness in a community
- skulls, weeds and ghosts are physical evidence of unwholesomeness, cognate with rotten
- language of play laced with 'carrion', 'guts', 'graves', 'worms', 'ulcers' and many gothic images of decay
- Ophelia, the pastoral maiden, is a victim of the rottenness of the court of Elsinore; her innocence is polluted by her father's and Claudius's obsession with sex, which also spreads to Gertrude and possibly Hamlet
- Claudius's fratricide, through poison in the ear, has spread to taint the whole state, as believed by the microcosm/macrocosm theory: Polonius, Rosencrantz and Guildenstern and Laertes have also become hypocritical, deceitful and self-serving
- some critics believe Hamlet is also tainted as he becomes mysogynistic, suspicious and violent – putting on an 'antic disposition' and behaving like those he criticises, changing from honesty to seeming
- Denmark can only be saved if the rottenness is excised by cleansing all the infected characters collaterally involved in the original, primeval, and deliberate act of evil

Further questions

2 '*Hamlet* is a world in which human life is held at nought.' What effect does this environment have on the action of the play?

3 Do you think it is valid to describe *Hamlet* as a play about Everyman, despite the particularity of the hero's circumstances?

4 Bradley described *Hamlet* as a 'tragedy of moral idealism'. Say what you think this means, and whether you agree.

5 Coleridge accused Hamlet of having 'an overbalance of the contemplative faculty'; in 'resolving to do everything, he does nothing' and so 'loses the power of action'. Do you agree that Hamlet thinks too much?

6 How successful is Shakespeare in creating (i) gothic atmosphere and (ii) the background of war in *Hamlet*, and to what dramatic use does he put them?

7 'The tragic hero of *Hamlet* is not the protagonist but the human race as a whole.' Explain this view and say whether you agree with it.

8 G. B. Shaw claimed 'Hamlet is not a single consistent character...he is half a dozen characters rolled into one.' Why do you think he said this, and do you agree?

9 'What captivates people is seeing human behaviour in a fix. Hamlet is given a task, but he is not a killer.' Is this an adequate summary of the fascination the play exerts over audiences?

10 C. S. Lewis said that 'the subject of *Hamlet* is death'. Explore this claim.

11 'Everything here is under-hand, meanly self-interested; nothing is frank or generous.' Is this a fair comment on Polonius and his son and daughter, and their family relationships?

12 What do we learn about the Elizabethan view of kingship from *Hamlet*?

13 'The action of *Hamlet* is no less than the Fall of Man, the failure of humanity.' Examine and evaluate this proposition.

14 Hamlet is 'the type of "modern" or post-Renaissance man: a man essentially divided within and against himself, and...necessarily at war with circumstance.' Discuss this description of Hamlet as a divided man at war.

15 'The essence of the tragic vision comes in the painful realisation of the distance between divine possibility and human aspiration.' How far does this apply to *Hamlet*?

16 'The central theme of *Hamlet* is Hamlet's inability to come to terms with reality.' Discuss this claim and say whether you agree.

17 'There's a divinity that shapes our ends/Rough hew them how we will.' How does this statement by Hamlet reflect his experience in the play?

18 Dr Johnson described Ophelia as 'the young, the beautiful, the harmless, and the pious'. Do you agree with this eulogistic description?

19 As a director, how would you wish to present Claudius in a production of the play? In the course of your answer:
- Explain clearly those aspects of Claudius's character that you would want to emphasise.
- Comment on what the play suggests about Shakespeare's presentation of evil.

Passage-based essay questions

The question you choose may direct you to one or two prescribed passages or ask you to select your own. Either way you will need to show your knowledge of the whole play as well as your response to and analysis of particular sequences. Careful selection of passages is crucial to ensure the relevance and success of the essay. The passages you like or are most familiar with are not necessarily the most appropriate for a particular essay title. Do not waste time paraphrasing what happens in the scene or is being said in the speech; just give a quick summary of its setting and context, along the lines of who is present and why, what has just happened, what will follow, and what the dramatic purpose of it is.

Examiners advise that reference to the rest of the work should be as much as 60% of the essay even for a passage-based question. Focus closely on the passage(s) but also relate their content and/or language to elsewhere in the text, backwards and forwards, and link your comments to the overall themes and/or structure of the play. Include references to character, event, theme and language, and ask how the episode modifies or adds to our understanding so far, and how typical it is of the work as a whole. Think about reader/audience reaction, using your own as the basis for your response. In an open-book exam you will have the annotations you made in the margin and on the text, but only include the relevant ones, and remember that they need to be organised into a structured response, not just transferred to your essay as a list.

Passage-based questions: prescribed

1 Look again at Act IV scene 4. By a careful examination of this scene consider the importance of Shakespeare's presentation of the military context in which the action is set to your understanding of the play as a whole.

Specimen mark scheme:

AO1   Candidates will need to offer some definition of the 'military context' of the play: some will focus on the question of rank and the responsibilities attaching to it, particularly in times of war; others will consider the attitudes and approaches to life a military life inculcates and expects.

AO2ii The question requires candidates to consider the scene in the context of the play as a whole; the quality of comparison they offer with the rest of the play will depend on the range of different aspects of the military context which they identify in the prescribed scene, from the respective positions of Hamlet, Laertes and Fortinbras, to the sense of measure which informs their behaviour.

AO3   The key word here is 'presentation'; at the bottom end answers are likely to focus on action and characterisation, while at the top they are likely to consider the importance of structure and the parallels and resonances this sets up.

AO4   The question presents candidates with an angle on the text to which to respond; quality of argument will be a significant discriminator here, with some candidates simply asserting the importance of the military context, while others assess its relative importance, possibly suggesting that other elements are more vital to an understanding of the play as a whole.

AO5ii The question invites direct consideration of the importance of the military context and candidates are likely also to consider the importance of the national and personal dimension; what will distinguish them here will be the extent to which they consider the influence of the external Elizabethan military, political and social context on the play, and the impact of their own historical, cultural, and social perspective on their response to the play.

Further questions

2 Remind yourself of the ending of the play from the beginning of the fencing match (Claudius: 'Set me the stoups of wine upon that table') to Hamlet's death ('the rest is silence'). What might the thoughts and feelings of an audience be as they watch this sequence? You should show an awareness of the characteristics of dramatic climax and Shakespearean tragedy.

3 Look at Act II scene 2, line 546 to the end of the scene. What does this show us about Hamlet's state of mind at this point in the play? Referring closely to the speech, show how his mood changes as the speech progresses.

4 Look again at Act III scene 4, starting at the beginning with Polonius: ''A will come straight. Look you lay home to him.' What effect do Hamlet's and Gertrude's words and actions in this scene have on your thoughts and feelings towards both of them?

5 Look again at Ophelia's report to Polonius about her private scene with Hamlet. Write about the significance of the passage, concentrating on the revelation of characters and the play's central themes.

6   What is a man,
       If his chief good and market of his time
       Be but to sleep and feed? (*Hamlet* IV.4.33–35)

Comment on the significance of this question and its connection to the preoccupations of the play and its central character.

7 Remind yourself of the events of Act I. In what ways does the first act prepare the audience for what is to follow? Look at themes, images, language, characters and relationships.

8 Look again at the graveyard scene (V.1) and the dialogue between Hamlet and First Clown and Hamlet and Horatio (lines 115 to 213). What do the setting, dramatic situation and content of the speeches add to the themes and atmosphere of the play?

9 Turn to Act IV scene 5 and remind yourself of the section from the beginning of the scene to Ophelia's exit (around line 74). Bearing in mind your knowledge of the whole play, what do you find of dramatic interest and significance in this extract, and what effect does it have on the audience?

10 Look at Act I scene 3 and describe the purpose and effect of this scene at this stage in the play.

11 'Shakespeare reveals in *Hamlet* a preoccupation with death which is almost an obsession.' Do you agree with this view? You should include in your answer material from Act V scene 2.

12 A modern critic has questioned why 'it seems to have become necessary, in order to keep our sympathy for the hero, to shift the burden of blame from Hamlet to Gertrude'. Explore Shakespeare's presentation of Gertrude in the light of this critical opinion, including in your answer some examination of Act III scene 4.

13 'In the last scene, Hamlet changes from philosophical questionings to acceptance of his fate — and this is the moment when Shakespeare presents him as ceasing to be superior to those around him.' What is your response to this critical judgement? Include in your answer some discussion of Act V scene 2 (up to the entrance of Osrick).

14   KING: ...this vile deed
       We must with all our majesty and skill
       Both countenance and excuse. (Act IV scene 1 lines 30–32)

Explore Shakespeare's presentation of control and manipulation in the play, including in your answer an examination of Act IV scene I and at least one other extract of your own choice.

15 'In the world Shakespeare presents in *Hamlet*, it is impossible to make moral judgements with certainty.' Do you agree? In your answer you should include an examinaton of Act III scene 3.

16 One critical judgement of the play is that 'Hamlet has no stable identity in a disjointed society which is full of contradictions.' Explore the significance of Hamlet's search for identity in the play as a whole, using as part of your answer your examination of the end of Act II scene 2 (from 'Now I am alone', line 546).

17 Using a detailed examination of Act I scene I as a starting point, explore the uses Shakespeare makes of historical conflict in the play as a whole.

Passage-based questions: selected

1 Select and analyse a sequence which reveals Hamlet's attitude towards female sexuality.

Possible ideas for a plan:

- use nunnery scene, a diatribe against women as sexual beings, his two loved ones standing for the general frailty of women
- could also use end of closet scene when Hamlet lectures his mother on her sexual behaviour with Claudius and shows his disgust
- men afraid of cuckoldry and bastard children because they undermined all-important honour; women can't have honour, only reputation; public versus private dichotomy
- Eve's transgression; women as breeders of sinners; fickle and unfaithful
- standard attack on women at the time for using face paint to disguise and deceive; women's beauty men's downfall, so viewed with suspicion
- Hamlet seems to have a romantic view of women in the letter to Ophelia, and again at her funeral; contradiction inherent in society and relevant to Hamlet's character
- his view of women changed by his mother's o'erhasty remarriage, and his realisation that both are sexual beings and therefore dangerous
- social background of women seen as either virgins or whores, nothing between the two, church-sanctioned misogyny
- his attacks on Ophelia and Gertrude for selling their bodies stem from perceived disloyalty to him (loss of throne, return of letters), and complicated in both cases by his need to score against the women's male minders (Polonius and Claudius)
- still loves desexualised, idealised versions of two women and is concerned for their moral and spiritual status

Further questions

2 A director has described the play as 'full of muddle. Hamlet doesn't know what to do next.' Refer to two passages which prove or disprove this accusation against Hamlet.

3 To what extent do you agree that in *Hamlet* Shakespeare presents 'women as destroyers of men'? You should base your answer on a close examination of two or more appropriate sequences of your choice.

4 G. Wilson Knight claimed that 'Hamlet denies the existence of romantic values' and takes a 'devilish joy' in being cruel and cynical. With reference to at least two passages, support or refute this critic's assessment of the character of Hamlet.

5 Audiences are sympathetic to Hamlet because of his sarcastic wit. Refer to two or three passages which reveal this characteristic and discuss its significance to the play as a whole.

6 Choose a particular scene or self-contained section of the play and give a full analysis of it, commenting on what it reveals about characters and themes; its dramatic effect; its use of language; and anything else which interests you.

7 Dr Johnson said that 'we must allow to the tragedy of *Hamlet* the praise of variety'. Choose two scenes which exemplify variety in the play, and examine them.

8 In *Hamlet*, every character is an actor and every episode is a play. Discuss this claim with reference to two or three episodes.

9 'In Hamlet, Shakespeare creates a lying world which makes the audience doubt who or what to believe.' Your response to this view should include an examination of at least two extracts.

10 'In this play, Shakespeare dramatically demonstrates that revenge and justice are not compatible.' How do you interpret the presentation of 'revenge and justice' in *Hamlet*? You should include in your answer an examination of at least two appropriate extracts.

11 A critic has argued that the murder of old Hamlet by Claudius is 'the central symbol of corruption in the play'. Do you agree with this view? Your answer should refer to at least two extracts from the play.

12 Hamlet says 'What a piece of work is man!' but also 'man delights not me'. Do you agree that Shakespeare uses his dramatic presentation of the character of Hamlet to examine the complexity of human nature? You should refer to at least two appropriate extracts in your answer.

13 'Shakespeare creates in Hamlet a character who is a prince yet who has no power.' In the light of this quotation explore the role of Prince Hamlet within the play, referring to at least two extracts.

14 'Whilst old King Hamlet lived in a medieval world of trial by combat, young Prince Hamlet lives in Claudius's more modern court.' In the light of this judgement, explore the ways in which Shakespeare presents the clash of cultures and views within the play as a whole. In your answer you should include reference to two or more appropriate sequences.

15 How do you respond to Shakespeare's presentation of the impact of Christian belief in *Hamlet*? Base your answer on a detailed examination of at least two appropriate sequences.

Sample essays

Below are two sample essays of different types written by different students. Both of them have been assessed as falling within the top band. You can judge them against the Assessment Objectives for this text for your exam board and decide on the mark you think each deserves and why. You may also be able to see ways in which each could be improved in terms of content, style and accuracy.

Sample essay 1

Consider *Hamlet* as an example of revenge tragedy, paying attention to Hamlet's own thoughts about his task and how Shakespeare's audience might have responded.

The English theatre sources were found in the medieval miracle and morality plays. Revenge tragedies were first performed at religious festivals, and as secular drama developed companies of travelling players put on performances in a village inn or manor house, castle or palace. They had their origin in the works of the Roman playwright Seneca, in which bloodshed is purged by more bloodshed, and is fatal to the avenger himself. He is often urged on by ghosts in a generally doom-laden atmosphere full of inevitability, in which horror is piled upon horror. The plots of revenge tragedies take precedence over the characters. The English plays which imitated Seneca's style were more dramatic but less rhetorical. The earliest significant example is *Gorboduc* (1561) and the most famous early play is *The Spanish Tragedy* by Thomas Kyd, who it is believed may have written an earlier version of *Hamlet*.

Shakespeare's *Hamlet* is the ultimate revenge tragedy in having all the ingredients required: the supernatural, incest, revenge, damnation, and providence. It also has two kinds of madness, the affected madness of Hamlet and the actual madness of Ophelia. However, the play has added subtlety not normally found in a revenge tragedy in that Hamlet is a Christian prince whose doubts and scruples stand in the way of action. He knows that killing is forbidden by the scriptures and that following an instruction from a ghost puts his soul at risk. When he first encounters the ghost he follows it instinctively because it looks like his father, but he is also aware that it may be bringing 'blasts from hell'. He refuses to kill Claudius at prayer not only because he thinks it would not count as true revenge, but also because he is not prepared, as Laertes allegedly is, to cut someone's throat in a church, which would guarantee his own damnation.

We get an insight into Hamlet's concerns about his own soul through his soliloquies. Though he would like not to have to delay, to be over and done with his task, his procrastination is for his own protection. He envies both the First Player and Horatio for opposite reasons: the former can perform any action in a dream of passion, because he inhabits a fictional world without consequences, and the latter is so far from being 'passion's slave' that he is unmoved by any irrational suggestion. Hamlet also shows concern for the souls of his two loved ones, Ophelia and his mother, in the nunnery scene and the closet scene respectively. He makes scathing comments about Laertes and Fortinbras, who represent stereotypical revenge tragedy protagonists and are only interested in fighting, quarrelling and their personal honour, vaunting themselves as heroes and showing no concern for their followers. For them morality is as fragile as an 'eggshell' and of no value.

Eventually Hamlet realises that 'all occasions do inform against me and spur my dull revenge'; he accepts that he has been chosen as a divine agent and he must bow to his inevitable task of carrying out justice on Claudius and purging Denmark of evil. He no longer resists his fate and allows himself to be led away to England, trusting that a 'cherub' will guide him. The Ghost has been supplanted by providence, and he does not mention it, or his father, again. Although already a killer and about to commit more murders, Hamlet has moved up to a higher level, of acting out heaven's purposes, not his own.

What Shakespeare achieves in *Hamlet* is the amalgamation of a popular barbaric genre of play, with a gothic setting and plenty of blood, guts and melodrama to please the masses, with a sophisticated and realistic main character capable of complexity and subtle psychological insight. Instead of simply being satisfied with the expected and necessary outcome of the avenger dying in order to carry out of his revenge, Shakespeare's audience may have felt some pity for the sensitive, suffering young man who did not choose or enjoy his role and who was very aware of the moral issues and what was at stake personally. They would still, however, have expected him to fulfil his mission as a dutiful son and a royal prince for whom *noblesse oblige*.

Sample essay 2

How important is the Ghost in *Hamlet*? Consider the viewpoint of both the original audience and a modern one.

Hamlet is one of Shakespeare's most supernatural plays. The characters and plot are complex and the ambiguities confuse and excite the audience. The Ghost in particular has this effect. It is not possible to know whether Shakespeare believed in ghosts, but he obviously knew their value in the theatre. Though only seen twice, the Ghost is essential to the play; as Dover Wilson says: 'The Ghost is the linchpin of *Hamlet*; remove it and the play falls to pieces.' Its relevance is not only confined to the plot and the creation of drama, suspicion and suspense, but to the raising of religious differences and thematic issues.

Shakespeare establishes the authenticity of the Ghost from the outset, and unlike Banquo's ghost in *Macbeth* it cannot be considered as a figment of the protagonist's imagination. The play begins with the scholarly Horatio having been brought to the battlements at midnight to witness 'this apparition come'. Horatio, a sceptic, responds 'Tush, tush 'twill not appear', which leads the audience to also doubt that it will, so the effect is stronger when it actually does, proving that we humans can't be sure of anything. However, the nature of the Ghost is not yet revealed and thus Shakespeare plays upon the conflicting attitudes towards spirits of his Elizabethan audience. A modern one would be less divided and more inclined to assume malevolent intent, as that is how ghosts have been presented in the centuries since.

The religious situation in England during Shakespeare's time was uncertain. Although the Protestant Elizabeth, daughter of Henry VIII, had been on the throne for over 40 years, there had been Catholic plots against her during her reign, most notably that of her rival

Mary Queen of Scots, and her successor was expected to be Mary's son, James VI of Scotland. It is not known where Shakespeare's religious leanings lay, but it has been widely speculated that his father John was sympathetic to 'the old religion', i.e. Catholicism. Catholics believed that ghosts might be the spirits of the departed, allowed to return from purgatory for a special purpose, which it was the duty of the receiver of the visitation to achieve in order to gain release and rest for the wandering and suffering soul. Protestants, however, feared all apparitions as they were deemed to be either damned spirits or devils assuming the guise of relatives in order to harm those to whom they appeared.

Shakespeare demonstrates both these views, using Horatio and the soldiers as well as Hamlet himself as mouthpieces, and thus creates a serious element of doubt in the play, for the audience and Hamlet, by his introduction of such an ambiguous figure. We are tricked, as the soldiers are, into believing the Ghost's visitation is to do with the unsettled times for Denmark and it comes as a shock to learn several scenes later that it has a different purpose. Horatio then warns that it may make Hamlet mad and tempt him to suicide, and immediately after meeting it Hamlet does affect madness (and some critics believe really becomes mad) and continues to toy with a death wish. The suspense and tension is wound up by Hamlet's need to test the Ghost and discover whether it is good or evil, 'a spirit of health or goblin damned'. Though his first instinct is to believe that it is his father's spirit, he later worries that 'the devil hath power to assume a pleasing shape'. Hamlet's essential dilemma, from which the others all stem, originates in the appearance of the Ghost, and the audience are forced to battle with uncertainty along with the hero. For a good half of the play Hamlet is in doubt about the Ghost's authenticity and only after the Mousetrap is he willing to say 'I'll take the ghost's word for a thousand pound'.

Of course, without the Ghost a simple but essential plot function would be missing: the knowledge of Claudius's evil deed. In addition, it could be interpreted that by disobeying the Ghost's injunction and speaking severely to his mother he sets off a chain of events which inevitably culminate in his own death: his mother's appeal for help causes the cry of Polonius, causing the death of Polonius, causing Hamlet to become the object of Claudius's death plot and Laertes's vengeance. That the Ghost reappears in the closet scene does suggest that he is annoyed by Hamlet's attack on his mother – not realising that he is trying to save her blackened soul by being cruel only to be kind – and by Hamlet's 'blunted purpose'. He thus has a judgemental role in addition to all his others, and it seems a case of 'like father like son' that Hamlet also takes it upon himself to judge others and find them wanting. The Ghost is also a reminder of the old code of chivalry and honour, with its settling of national disputes by single combat, which Hamlet is ambivalent about but has to live up to.

Modern audiences find it difficult to forgive the Ghost his imperiousness and callous-ness towards his son. He makes no apology for asking Hamlet to break one of the ten commandments, for his own personal satisfaction; he does not suggest that Claudius is a bad ruler of Denmark. The direct accomplishment of his dread command would certainly lead

to the damnation of Hamlet. Fortunately the performing of the murder is finally indirect and unplanned (the means not provided by him), which saves Hamlet from divine punishment. However, because they do not have the same belief in ghosts and religious scruples as contemporary audiences, modern spectators are likely to attribute Hamlet's indecision and delay more to his character traits of melancholy and conscience than to real doubt about the nature of ghosts and the necessity of following their instructions. However the Ghost is presented on stage (and there have been many forms and special effects tried over the centuries, from it being invisible to it being a colossal statue) it should be impressive, as it is the first performer to an audience in a play about performing to an audience and it initiates all the multiple applications and ironies of the theme of acting, among others.

Further study

For a note on the editions of *Hamlet* referred to and their introductions, see 'Play context' on pp. 18–21.

Books

Bradley, A. C. (1904) *Shakespearean Tragedy*, Penguin.

Clemen, W. (1951) *The Development of Shakespeare's Imagery*, Harvard University Press.

Coyle, M. (ed.) (1992) *Hamlet: A Casebook*, Macmillan.

Empson, W. (1995) *The Structure of Complex Words*, Penguin.

Hawkes, T. (ed.) (1969) *Coleridge on Shakespeare*, Penguin Shakespeare Library.

Honigmann, E. A. J. (1976) *Shakespeare: Seven Tragedies*, Macmillan.

Honigmann, E. A. J. (1989) *Myriad-Minded Shakespeare*, Macmillan.

Jones, E. (1976) *Hamlet and Oedipus*, Norton.

Jump, J. D. (ed) (1968) *Hamlet: A Selection of Critical Essays* (Casebook series), Macmillan.

Kermode, F. (2001) *Shakespeare's Language*, Penguin.

Knight, G. W. (2001) *The Wheel of Fire*, Routledge.

Knights, L. C. (1960) *An Approach to 'Hamlet'*, Chatto and Windus.

Leech, C. (1969) *Tragedy* (The Critical Idiom series, ed. John Jump), Routledge.

Lerner, L. (ed.) (1970) *Shakespeare's Tragedies*, Penguin.

Levin, H. (1970) *The Question of 'Hamlet'*, Oxford University Press.

Mahood, M. M. (1968) *Shakespeare's Wordplay*, Methuen.

Muir, K. (1972) *Shakespeare's Tragic Sequence*, Hutchinson University Library.

Muir, K. (1987) *Shakespeare's 'Hamlet'* (Studies in English Literature), Hodder Arnold.

Prosser, E. (1972) *'Hamlet' and Revenge*, Stanford University Press.

Rossiter, A. P. (1989) *Angel with Horns: 15 Lectures on Shakespeare*, Longman.

Shapiro, J. (2005) *1599: A Year in the Life of William Shakespeare*, Faber.

Spurgeon, C. F. E. (1935) *Shakespeare's Imagery and What It Tells Us*, Cambridge University Press.

Tillyard, E. M. W. (1998) *The Elizabethan World Picture*, Pimlico.

Waldock, A. J. A. (1981) *'Hamlet': A Study in Critical Method*, Sydney University Press.

Wilson, E. (ed) (1969) *Shaw on Shakespeare*, Penguin.

Essays

Eliot, T. S. (1919) 'Hamlet' in *Selected Essays* (1975), Faber.

Eliot, T. S. (1932) 'Hamlet and his Problems' in *Selected Essays* (1975), Faber.

Knight, G. W. (1930) 'The Embassy of Death: An Essay on *Hamlet*' in *The Wheel of Fire* (2001), Routledge.

Lewis, C. S. (1942) 'Hamlet: the Prince or the Poem' in *Selected Literary Essays* (1969), Cambridge University Press.

Films

Hamlet has not surprisingly proved a popular subject for film makers from the birth of the industry; it has been described as the world's most filmed tragic story. In the summer of 1994 the National Film Theatre season featured 12 *Hamlets* and there are at least 50 in existence. No fewer than four silent black and white versions were made between 1907 and 1922, and at least another 15 films have been made since then in English alone. Particularly memorable productions include:

1948: directed by Lawrence Olivier, who also took the part of Hamlet

1964: directed by John Gielgud; Richard Burton played Hamlet

1969: directed by Tony Richardson; Nicol Williamson played Hamlet

1980: directed by Rodney Bennett; Derek Jacobi played Hamlet

1990: directed by Franco Zeffirelli; Mel Gibson played Hamlet

1996: directed by Kenneth Branagh, who also took the part of Hamlet [note: there are two versions of the video of this production: one is cut to 2 hours, the other is the full 4-hour version]

Rosencrantz and Guildenstern are Dead is an ironic and amusing play by Tom Stoppard derived from *Hamlet*; it offers a new perspective on Shakespeare's play and draws attention to its paradoxes, themes and imagery. There is a film version, directed by Stoppard himself (1990).

Internet

There are now a vast number of sites on the internet with useful material on Shakespeare and *Hamlet*; a Google search for "Hamlet" returns 22,000,000 pages, although not all are useful.

http://shakespeare.palomar.edu (Mr William Shakespeare and the Internet) is one of the best general Shakespeare sites. It includes general information and an extensive set of links to other sites, many of which include the full text of some or all of the plays, listed at http://shakespeare.palomar.edu/works.htm. Most of these have some form of search engine which allows the text to be searched for words or phrases. www.eamesharlan.org/tptt/ is one which includes a word count, and line count by character, for each play.

As far as *Hamlet* is concerned, in addition to sections in or referred to in the sites above, there are a number of individual sites worthy of note:

- www.sparknotes.com/shakespeare/hamlet/ is a good introductory site, with the full text, notes and search engine.
- Another good introductory site is www.absoluteshakespeare.com/guides/hamlet/hamlet.htm.
- The University of Victoria has texts of the Quarto and Folio at www.ise.uvic.ca/Library/plays/Ham.html, accessible by scene or by page.
- There is a good collection of essays on *Hamlet* at www.shakespeare-online.com/essays/hamletessays.html.
- 'Hamlet on the Ramparts' (see Penguin introduction, p. lxxx) is at: http://shea.mit.edu/ramparts/.
- The legally annotated Hamlet website by Mark Alexander is to be found at: www.shakespearefellowship.org/virtualclassroom/Law/legalhamlet/.
- An interesting essay by Margaret Atwood is www.web.net/owtoad/ophelia.html.

Other useful websites:
- www.shakespeares-globe.org is the official website of the reconstructed Globe Theatre.
- www.shakespeare.org.uk is the site of the Shakespeare Birthplace Trust.